Everyday Business Etiquette

Everyday Business Etiquette

Marilyn Pincus

DEDICATION

This book is dedicated to my wonderful daughters and sons named here in the order of their arrival—Arlene, Steven, Karen, Joseph, Alan, and Rebecca.

ACKNOWLEDGMENTS

My sincere thanks to Ms. Grace E. Freedson, Managing Editor and Director of Acquisitions, Barron's, for guidance, inspiration, and cheerful optimism!

Although this book has only one author, it takes a collaboration of effort to bring a book to life. My thanks to the many skilled and talented people associated with Barron's whose work contributed to make this book possible and to those individuals who see to it the book is well traveled and enjoys longevity. Surely my good manners would be in doubt if I did not specifically recognize Ms. Anna E. Damaskos, General Editor.

All inquiries should be addressed to:
Barron's Educational Series, Inc.
250 Wireless Boulevard
Hauppauge, New York 11788

International Standard Book No. 0-8120-9517-0

Library of Congress Catalog Card No. 96-18528

Library of Congress Cataloging-in-Publication Data
Pincus, Marilyn.
Everyday business etiquette / by Marilyn Pincus.
p. cm.
Includes index.
ISBN 0-8120-9517-0
1. Business etiquette. I. Title.
HF5389.P58 1996
395′.52—dc20 96-18528
CIP

PRINTED IN THE UNITED STATES OF AMERICA

987654321

CONTENTS

Foreword

We are crossing the threshold of a new millennium. What an earthshaking, historic occasion of monumental importance! Yet, where are the cries of joy and celebration throughout the land? Are we so uptight, worried about safety and the environment, distressed about our children and fearful of economic insecurity that we can't look to the promise of the next millennium with great anticipation?

Perhaps the answer to the dilemma of advanced technology is that we have lost much of our humanity in marching forward with our wondrous machines. We spend so much time manipulating a mouse and pushing space bars, keys and buttons, we don't have time for human conversation or an awareness of the *people* around us.

Most parents today, particularly single and dual-career parents, don't have the time to teach civility to their children the way they learned it from their parents and grandparents. There isn't the time to talk to the younger generation about the nuances of proper behavior, nor is there the desire of the young to learn them. Each generation comes home at night to absent itself with its own devices and its own agenda. Dad's on the fax, Mom's on the cellular phone, junior's destroying the universe with his computer game and little Suzy is on-line, chatting with someone about Barbie dolls. We don't seem to have the time to imprison our children at the dinner table, teaching them manners, compassion, conversation and a thousand other good things.

Civility is fading away from us, and it shows up more clearly in the workplace than anywhere else (with the exception of the way people drive their cars on the freeways and on crowded city streets.) Marilyn Pincus is a fighter for civility. She knows that success in business depends as much on the human element and people skills as it does on a person's dexterity with a mouse and spreadsheets. People ask me why I'm always plugging the competition—other peoples' books and articles on manners. The answer is simple. Our society is in trouble, and we need every bit of help we can get. That's why I hope Marilyn Pincus's book will enjoy success.

Letitia Baldrige

Introduction: Your Passport to Success

All interpersonal relationships are guided by widely accepted rules regarding what is and what is not appropriate behavior. Etiquette, courtesy, good manners, grace, savoir-faire, refinement, gentility, decorum, and deportment are simple words used to describe the positive results of actions which aren't always simple to chart. Should I or shouldn't I? What's correct? What's offensive? What's expected? Did I make a mistake?

Interpersonal relationships in the business world pose a special challenge because the consequences of a faux pas can be far-reaching (e.g., a lost sale, an angry customer who speaks ill of you to others, a dissatisfied boss, a missed opportunity). Moreover, there's a tendency to excuse someone you love if they hurt your feelings or to be forgiven by a friend if you break the rules of etiquette, but forgiveness is a rare commodity in the business world.

Consequently, business experts have put the spotlight on business etiquette and much has been written about the rules.

Everyday Business Etiquette is as different from other business etiquette books as day is from night. In addition to announcing current do's and don'ts, *Everyday Business Etiquette* offers background and support for the individual who recognizes that it takes more than a mastery of the rules to prosper in the business arena.

Here's a privileged look at what's going on but isn't immediately evident to everyone.

FORM AND FUNCTION

Business life is filled with variations on a theme. You may, for example, memorize rules about who should be introduced to whom and in what order. All of a sudden, however, you're charged with making introductions and one executive in the group is wearing dark glasses, has a guide dog at his side, and is apparently challenged by a low-vision or no-vision handicap.

How should you proceed?

Do the accepted rules for making an introduction still apply?

In all the years you'll be called upon to make introductions, this kind of challenge may never again arise.

Even if you were willing to memorize all rules of etiquette that were ever documented, do you think you'd find a rule to govern this situation? Not likely.

You know how to make introductions. In other words, you know the form.

But . . .

What is the function of the introductions . . . the purpose, use, reason for, aim, intention, mission, design, point?

The boiled-down answer is that everyone present wants to be spotlighted.

Keep your mind on the function and proceed:

"Hal Burton, I'd like to introduce Mary Greer.

"Mr. Burton, Mary is standing to your left.

"Mary Greer is the editor of our employee newsletter and a member of our Communications Quality Team.

"Mary, Hal Burton has been with our parent company for fourteen years and is in charge of all telemarketing operations.

"Mr. Burton, permit me to introduce Jim Barstow and Martha Quinn.

"Jim Barstow and Martha Quinn comanage our night-shift customer-support operations."

SUBTLE MOVES

These introductions are made according to the rules with only a slight addition. There is a brief reference to where someone is standing. Assuming the sighted individuals are alert, they will each approach Hal Burton from his left side to shake hands. In this way, the handicap isn't an issue nor should it be one.

As you concentrate on form, maintain a measure of regard for function. Then, if and when form is challenged by the unexpected, you won't be stymied.

> *"Nothing contributes so much to tranquilize the mind as a steady purpose—a point on which the soul may fix its intellectual eye."*
>
> —Mary Wollstonecraft Shelley, 1818

This "steady purpose" focus is the backbone of this book and Part One, Strictly Business, (the first third of the book) has been specially crafted to address function and form. It makes this etiquette book unique and especially valuable. A concise, easy-to-understand presentation targets heart-of-the-matter information and serves to assist readers who must quickly prepare for "Special Times."

In command of *Everyday Business Etiquette* is where you want to be. You'll soon grasp the whys and wherefores of what you and others do concerning interpersonal relationships.

Combine know-why thinking with know-how skills and you'll enjoy a distinct advantage. You'll be able to act with confidence when you face interpersonal business challenges and you'll move forward with dispatch to achieve goals.

In effect, your command of *Everyday Business Etiquette* is your passport to success.

Part One

Strictly Business

1

Special Times: Get Ready, Get Set, Go!

Get Ready!

It's an age-old command that to this day is shouted in playgrounds when children are about to compete. You can bet that any worthy competitor you encounter, anywhere, pays heed to this command.

Preparation, or readiness, is a valuable key to success.

When you know in advance you're about to participate in a competition you have the luxury of time to get ready. Given sufficient time you can sharpen your know-how and put the odds of enjoying success in your favor.

Everyday Business Etiquette serves up customized information which has been boiled down for your quick and easy assimilation. It's the kind of information you need to be prepared to meet career-affecting challenges.

Remember, the business world thrives on competition.

You competed to win your job and you compete to hold your job. Your company competes to win and keep customers or clients. Every day, all kinds of goods and service providers compete for your money and even as one brand beckons to you, another tries to woo you away. Competitors are constantly jockeying to attain or maintain a winning position.

When you're promoted or have a new job within the company, you're walking in unfamiliar territory. You want to be at your best because there's always a rival waiting who would like to take your job!

When you occasionally travel to distant places to conduct business, or help to host dignitaries who are important to your company's success, you'll be called upon to act in new and different ways. You'll want to be at your best because your performance is closely tied to how well your company or your boss fares. If you should fall short of expectations, management is likely to be on the lookout for a more capable employee.

It's nothing personal.

Someone who counts you out isn't generally motivated by personal bias. It's a simple fact that sterling behavior is desirable, rewarded and helps you to carve out and keep your place in the winner's circle. Less-than-sterling behavior puts everyone at a disadvantage.

An excellent command of business etiquette, knowing what is correct and knowing how to behave at all times, enables you to position yourself up-front. Strive to be the best you can be and all contenders had better make way for you!

Get Set!

Review the following "Special Times" blueprints for success. If you're suddenly faced with a challenge, such as a request to entertain business people from another country, and you have some understanding of what may be expected and how to act and react, you'll feel your confidence level rise. Instead of feeling awkward and thinking "problem" when you observe these people coming through the door, you'll think "opportunity," and be ready to rise to the occasion.

When you know you'll soon confront a specific challenge (e.g., a job interview), turn to precise information to help you get ready. To best utilize this information:

- Adapt the blueprints to your circumstances.
- Visualize yourself following the guidelines; "rehearse" the situation.
- Use "spreadsheet" conjecture to evaluate results. "If I do this, then I can expect that. If that, then this."
- Fine-tune your plan.
- Read "On-the-Career-Path Tips." Strategies are explained and you'll be directed to not-to-be-missed chapters that discuss related topics. If, for example, it's the first time you'll be attending an industry convention you probably should read Chapter Three: Dining-Table Etiquette You Didn't Learn at Home and Chapter Ten: Introductions.

In no time at all, you'll be primed and ready to *Go!*

SEARCHING FOR YOUR FIRST FULL-TIME JOB

Your first full-time job probably coincides with school graduation. You, your friends, and your associates say goodby to one another and goodby to the comfortable corridors of education. Here, you know where you are, what's expected of you, and how to act to get desired responses. Soon you'll be interacting with people who aren't your instructors or buddies. Many of the rules that guided your relationships with professors and school friends won't apply in the business world. Most people know this, but they don't recognize that by *pinpointing* the differences, and the *significance* of those differences, they can be better prepared to function during their job-search.

If you're approaching your first full-time job search but aren't a recent school graduate (e.g., a member of the armed services, a homemaker), make an attempt to adapt the following observations to your circumstances. If that's not possible, disregard the A observations. Read the B observations to better understand the interviewee/interviewer relationship.

Note: Brief references to thank-you notes, résumés, and related subjects will be discussed in greater detail later.

Where You Are and Where You're Going: Comparisons

1-A. Teachers want you to succeed. It's a good reflection on them when you do well.

1-B. A company's representative who interviews job candidates wants to locate the best person for the job. He or she won't mind whether that's you or somebody else.

TO DO or not to do: Don't think of the interviewer as your ally. This is not the time to relax. It is the time to apply all the rules of business etiquette.

2-A. Teachers are expected to know *more* than students. Teachers are generally older than their students and normally positioned at least a few rungs above students on the who-deserves-our-respect-for-higher-achievement-ladder.

2-B. Interviewers may be the same age or younger than job-seekers. Interviewers will not normally have any know-how-to-do-it advantage regarding the job tasks you'll perform if you're hired.

TO DO or not to do: Don't assume someone your age will accord you special treatment because you have something in common. Do respond and extend the same courtesy to a young interviewer as you would any other interviewer. Don't adopt a you-know-more-than-I-do posture because the interviewer holds a position of authority. Toot your own horn, when appropriate, but maintain decorum.

3-A. Teachers usually spend a semester or more getting to know you before they judge you and give you grades.

3-B. Interviewers spend a relatively short time with you before they make a recommendation regarding whether or not to hire you.

TO DO or not to do: Recognize that you'd better get it right the first time. Your written résumé should look as good as it sounds. If a thank-you note is an appropriate follow-up to the interview meeting, you'd better know that and know how to produce it. Be prepared to demonstrate the proper measure of savoir-faire and you won't be inclined to inappropriately ingratiate yourself to the people in charge of hiring.

4-A. Teachers assume that students want to complete classes successfully and move forward. Goals are relatively clear.

4-B. Interviewers often ask what you want from the job and what salary you expect to earn. Your answers can automatically make you an unacceptable job candidate.

TO DO or not to do: Recognize that the ability to listen carefully is a cardinal rule of business etiquette. You'll probably spot clues that enable you to provide the kind of responses that will keep you in the game. Recognize that it's possible to diplomatically respond to a question with a question. This kind of know-how enables you to safely navigate muddy waters.

5-A. You have an expected path to follow in order to complete your education. The program is laid out for you. The instructors are in place. You have few choices to make as you move along to attain your diploma.

5-B. When you walk into a job interview, you have some expectations regarding the job description and your ability to perform but it's impossible to know precisely what is required.

TO DO or not to do: Once you suspect a job isn't for you, don't waste time. Notify the interviewer as tactfully as possible. Considerate people don't waste another person's time and your thoughtfulness should be appreciated. As a matter of fact, you wouldn't be the first person to arrive at a company seeking one job only to leave the premises hired to do a completely different job.

Okay. What Now?

When the spotlight shines on the world you're about to enter, it's easy to see you'll be called upon to change your modus operandi. More specifically, you've glimpsed at the interviewer/interviewee relationship and it's one that's about to occupy many of your waking hours.

> *"There is nothing so degrading as the constant anxiety about one's means of livelihood. . . . Money is like a sixth sense without which you cannot make a complete use of the other five."*
>
> William Somerset Maugham (*Of Human Bondage,* 1915)

One way to minimize your apprehensions, and apprehensions are natural for anyone about to make a major change, is to take control of the things you can control.

You'll be called upon to make snap decisions, react, and speak out based upon new sets of circumstances. You'll want your judgment to be sharp. You'll want to present yourself in the best possible light. Since it's not possible to know precisely which challenges you'll face (e.g. written tests, interview questions, meeting and greeting potential co-workers), you'll have to rely upon your general knowledge, life experiences, and specialized training to enable you to make appropriate responses.

Some challenges, however, only require advance planning. The more you prepare, the less you'll have to be concerned about when you're confronted with new conditions. Not only will you be more self-composed, you'll free yourself to concentrate on the new stuff since you've already taken control of the rest.

You're not likely to get a second chance to present yourself to your potential employer if you don't make a good first impression. Suppose you can't operate a popular software program that's prerequisite to obtaining this particular job. If you dazzle the interviewer with your over-all competence and enthusiasm, you may discover company management is willing to train you to operate the software program. They, too, must work to control the things they can control.

You've just uncovered a dynamite bit of information: *Control is a two-way street.*

- You can control your chances to succeed by being well prepared.
- A potential employer can't control everything. As a result, that individual may bend some rules to accommodate a potential employee who makes an impressive presentation.

After all, the employer can't control your appearance, your good manners, your ability to say and do the proper thing at the proper time. You make an offer the potential employer finds hard to refuse when you've got these attributes under control. Accordingly, this is the place to begin:

- Personal appearance
- Good manners
- Ability to say and do the right thing at the right time

Martin John Yate writes, "Even though the recent graduate must be taught most of the job's necessary skills, there are some he or she should bring to the table: Good listening, verbal and written skills, initiative, energy and an analytical approach to problems." (*Hiring the Best, A Manager's Guide,* Boston: Bob Adams, 1988.)

Remember

Another job candidate may present "all of the above" to the employer in addition to being able to operate that software program. That person is therefore likely to be the favored job candidate. Never allow a negative response to your request for a job make you feel negative. No successful person has ever ventured forth to achieve goals without meeting up with nay-sayers and disapproval along the way. A successful salesperson may be told "no" many times before hearing "yes."

All you need is one job . . . one "yes."

So if you meet up with a few no's, keep going. The "yes" may come today, or next month, but if you keep trying it will come.

What has this got to do with business etiquette?

This insight helps you to put a smile on your face and a bounce in your step. Smiles and a confident demeanor tend to put other people at ease.

A command of business etiquette helps you to put others at ease so that you can do business together.

Put it all together and you'll easily exude the energy and initiative Martin John Yate tells a manager to look for in order to "hire the best."

Personal Appearance

When you're properly dressed and groomed, you demonstrate respect and consideration for your surroundings and for those with whom you interact. If, for example, you want work in a bank, you'll arrive for your interview looking as though you belong in that environment. If the bank is located on Wall Street in New York City, you'll probably dress differently than if the bank is located on Broadway in Tucson, Arizona.

Since you're searching for your first full-time job, you may not own an interview outfit. If possible, plan to purchase or assemble more than one interview outfit. When a garment gets soiled and it requires a day or two to clean it, you won't be left unprepared to attend another interview. Moreover, if the company invites you back for a second interview, you'll be able to wear a different outfit.

Over-all grooming is important, too. Your hairstyle, attention to skin and nails, and choice of cosmetics all contribute to your appearance.

Be aware that your personal appearance sends a message before you have an opportunity to shake hands with your interviewer or answer any questions. Since almost everything about your personal appearance is within your control, you can give it the high priority it merits.

Good Manners

Résumé. Look at the résumé you prepared and answer the following questions. Do so even if an expert supervised the composition. The over-all appearance of this document will be judged along with the content.

1. *Is it neat? Neatness not only suggests that you're an orderly individual but that you have regard for the person who must take the time to read it. One experienced manager says, "A neat résumé or application form tells me a person is considerate."*
2. *Have you checked for accuracy? If, for example, you include personal references but don't use the person's correct title, you suggest a lack of*

respect for the individual's position, or, worse, that you may not know better. If the interviewer wishes to telephone you but you didn't provide your telephone area code with your number, you appear inconsiderate or careless.

Promptness. Don't be late for a meeting. Some business etiquette gurus suggest that being late for a meeting helps demonstrate power or gives you some kind of advantage. Other experts claim there's no excuse for being late. It suggests poor time-management skills and insinuates you don't think the other person's time is valuable. Years from today, when you're well-established in your career, you may choose to weigh the merits of the argument. Now, as you search for your first job, be on time, every time. If an emergency delays you, telephone the interviewer to explain your predicament. Be ready to reschedule the meeting if necessary, but don't make a new appointment if you're not sure you can keep it. It's more considerate to call back to confirm a proposed new meeting time and date than to cancel an appointment. If you do arrive late and the interviewer is willing to see you, courtesy demands that you apologize. Be assured, however, that you're not off to a good start when you arrive late.

If you arrive extra early, you may feel more relaxed if you wait in a nearby coffee shop or a downstairs lobby area and make your entrance a little before the scheduled hour. Do be on your best behavior wherever you go to wait. You never know who you're chatting with at the coffee shop or who may be watching you dunk your donut in your coffee, or your fingers into the cup to retrieve soggy pieces!

Handshakes and greetings. If you're asked to sit and wait for the interviewer, be prepared to rise when he or she enters the room. It's a courteous gesture and easy to execute. It also puts you in a better position for a handshake. Although most business greetings include a handshake, some people dispense with this formality. Take your cue from the interviewer.

If you shake hands, use a firm grip, and shake the person's hand once or twice. If only the two of you are present, introduce yourself to this individual as you shake his or her hand. "I'm Bob Grant. It's good to meet you." Or, "I've been looking forward to meeting you." A short statement is all that's required. If a third party makes the introduction, you needn't say anything, but do remember to smile.

Take note of the individual's name and use it occasionally as you speak. "I believe I got an excellent education in robotic sciences at Brayton University, Ms. Gray." Or, "I worked part-time during my four years of study, Mr. Rutledge, and so did my college friends."

It's a compliment to someone when you know and use his or her name and it's a help to you in remembering it if you contact or refer to this person at a future date. Which request sounds more intelligent? "I'd like to speak with the guy who interviewed me," or "Bob Rutledge, please."

If the room is large and you're seated far from the interviewer's desk, you may want to take a seat closer to the person. If you're not invited to do so, ask for permission to do so. In addition to being able to hear better and to speak in normal tones, it will make it comfortable for you to make eye contact. When you make eye contact you'll find it easier to give the interviewer your undivided attention. You'll also appear alert and interested and that works to your benefit.

Avoid "me-isms." A courteous individual thinks about how his or her actions affect others. He or she doesn't say "I" and "me" too often. An interview setting, however, is designed for you to talk about yourself and your accomplishments. Take care to attach what you say to the company and the company's needs as much as possible. In order to do this, it's important to know about the company before you arrive for an interview. This strategy should continue to work well for you throughout your career. The more you learn about a customer's needs, for example, the more you'll be able to fulfill those needs.

"Think the way the birds think," is an old advertising dictum. When you respond to questions, you should "think the way the interviewer thinks." Let him or her know about your skills and abilities in light of what the company needs. You can ask questions, too. Find out all you can about the specific job. Then, instead of saying, "I'm great. I can do it," you'll be able to say, "My part-time work at a car dealership gave me direct sales experience. My training should come in handy, if I join your telemarketing department."

Ability To Say and Do the Right Thing

In James A. Autry's 1994 book, *Life & Work A Manager's Search For Meaning,* (NY: William Morrow), he raises the issue of managers wanting to do the right thing but asking, "Just what is the right thing?"

You'll probably agree there's no easy answer to the question. An answer would presume we know everything there is to know about anything we may have to confront. That's not possible.

When Autry later asks, "What will I not do ever?", he makes it easier to respond.

In part, your ability to say and do the right thing stems from knowing what you won't do.

What You Won't Do

You'll want to be as cooperative as possible with interviewers and company representatives when you're searching for your first full-time job.

What happens, however, if the interviewer is rude?

She may keep you waiting beyond the agreed upon meeting time without explanation. She may not introduce herself to you. Your responses to her questions may be interrupted by the frequent telephone calls she accepts. When she doesn't make eye contact, you don't know if she's paying attention to you.

Don't allow anyone's inconsiderate behavior to mar your performance. Respond to this rude individual as though she were *etiquette-correct*. You'll say and do the right thing because you wouldn't think of doing otherwise.

In today's marketplace, some companies have adapted a policy of testing all prospective employees for drug use. No doubt management wouldn't elect to adopt a drug-testing policy without what they perceive to be valid reasons. At the least, it costs money to administer the tests and creates paperwork and record-keeping chores. When you know in advance that you may be asked to submit to a drug test, consider carefully how to respond.

Compliance may not be the right decision for you. You may never take illegal drugs but you may feel the company's policy is offensive and you're not sure you want the job if it requires drug-testing.

You'll probably learn about a drug-testing policy from signs posted in the personnel office or from a release form you're expected to sign that accompanies the job application. On the chance that you're unaware of this prerequisite until late in the process and an interview is underway, you may want to ask the interviewer to permit you to take the release form or any other papers you're expected to sign home with you. You can promise to mail the signed papers to the office or return them yourself.

Since some explanation is probably necessary, you might volunteer that your attorney insists you not sign any agreements until he or she reviews them.

If you leave the interviewer thinking you're the executor of a fabulous estate or hold some exalted position in your private life and that's why you have legal counsel, no harm should be done.

On the chance that you later decide to pursue a job at this company, you'll return to the scene with a clean slate.

This alert is intended to illustrate how you can say and do the right thing even when you feel annoyed or unsure.

You can always handle yourself with decorum.

A Sign of the Times

If you don't engage in a face-to-face interview with a person but rather with a mechanism, don't despair.

According to Elizabeth Oberbeck's Job Strategies column (*Glamour,* February 1995), "New interviewing techniques . . . can be impersonal and intimidating for job hunters." She discusses the video interview, the electronic interview, and the gang-up interview, all of which sound daunting. Whether you face a computer screen, respond to questions via touch-tone telephone, or face a video camera when you respond to questions, the techniques that serve you best under more traditional conditions will work for you now.

The gang-up interview? That's when instead of interacting with one interviewer, you interact with two or more questioners.

Keep in mind that modern-day tools may come and go, but the people skills and techniques that are prized when individuals perform in the workplace are timeless. You've got them under control!

ON-THE-CAREER-PATH TIPS

- Read Chapter Two: The Finer Points of Interview Etiquette
- Read Chapter Seven: Send A Message With Your Wardrobe Selections

AND

- For more how-to information pertaining to your appearance read *Projecting a Positive Image.* This 105-page, Business Success Series title was published by Barron's in 1993 and is available at major book stores and some libraries.
- If you want to put your best foot forward, it's good form to mail a short thank-you note to the interviewer within 24 hours of the meeting.

The following sample letters can be used or adapted to meet your needs. Give your finished letter the ten-point checkup on page 174, Chapter Twelve: Correspondence, before you put it in the mailbox.

Your name
Address
City, State, Zip Code
Telephone Number
(with area code)

Date

Interviewer's full name
Title (e.g., Director of Human Resources)
Framingham Steel
Address
City, State, Zip Code

Dear Mr. Rutledge:

I enjoyed meeting with you this morning. I left your office feeling enthusiastic about the possibility of working for Framingham Steel. I feel certain I can make a valuable contribution to the company's prosperity.

It would be my pleasure to learn I've been chosen to participate in the next Junior Executive Training Session at Framingham Steel.

Thank you for your time and consideration.

Sincerely,

Judith Morney

Your name
Address
City, State, Zip Code
Telephone number
(with area code)

Date

Interviewer's full name
Title (e.g., Director of Human Resources)
Carlson Industries
Address
City, State, Zip Code

Dear Ms. Badgers:

I'd be pleased to be able to say, "I work for Carlson Industries."

It's obvious to me that Carlson employees take pride in every finished product they send to the marketplace and Carlson Industries' customers receive superior service.

I'm ready, willing, and able to work to perpetuate these winning practices. Thank you.

Sincerely,

John Patrick Heigh

Your name
Address
City, State, Zip Code
Telephone number
(with area code)

Date

Interviewer's full name
Title (e.g., Director of Human Resources)
TBA Manufacturing
Address
City, State, Zip Code

Dear Mr. Lyons:

As you know, Ralph Berks gave me a tour of the main plant. I've already thanked Mr. Berks for sharing his time and knowledge with me.

The tour confirmed my belief that my training and work experience prepare me to complement your plant management team. I recognize the importance of an uninterrupted work flow at the main plant and assure you if you offer me this position, I'll exceed your performance expectations from day one!

Thank you.

Sincerely,

Phil Riggs

 STRATEGY YOU CAN USE

Answer-a-Question-with-a-Question Strategy. To avoid having to make a direct response when you feel unprepared to answer, ask questions and try to obtain more information. Or lead the interrogator in a different direction. The following snippets of conversation illustrate the strategy. The questions are patterned after actual interview questions.

Manager: Now that you've earned your college degree do you feel you have anything else to learn?

Candidate: I think all of life is a learning process, don't you?

Goal: The candidate answers politely but since he doesn't know why the manager asks such a question, the candidate fishes for more input by tagging on his own question.

Personnel Director: Can you ignore what you learned at school and accept what you learn on the job?

Candidate: Don't you believe my formal education is an asset?

Goal: The Director's inference could be perceived as rude, but the candidate maintains her poise. Then, too, the question could be an attempt at levity. The candidate wants to discover why, or if, the interviewer holds her college or her achievements in low regard. In this way, she'll know better how to proceed. Perhaps the Director isn't aware that the institution of which she is an alumna is an excellent one, and the candidate should speak to that fact. Or it may be the interviewer is biased about the merits of on-the-job training. It behooves the candidate to find out more before she responds.

Executive: Where else are you applying for a job?

Candidate: As you can imagine, I want a job where I can use my skills to the best advantage. I'm concentrating my search on the publishing industry.

Note: This example represents a strategy variation. The candidate didn't pose a question but didn't specifically answer the question either. If the executive persists, the candidate will have to decide whether or not he's violating confidentiality by answering directly. Here are some options:

Candidate: I've made application to several other firms.

Candidate: I have one firm job offer but haven't accepted it, yet. I wanted to meet with you first. I don't think it's proper for me to mention the other company name, do you?

Boss: Where do you see yourself six months from now?

Candidate: Isn't this job a long-term job?

Goal: Is the boss wondering whether the candidate is serious about a permanent position and concerned about spending time and money to train this person? Or does he want to know if he's a go-getter and expects to move up in the company? It's proper for the candidate to supply a direct answer but easier to give the answer the boss is looking for once more is known.

RETURNING TO THE WORKPLACE AFTER A LONG HIATUS

If you're returning to the workforce after a company downsizing left you out in the cold and searching for a new position, congratulations! Experts tell us that finding a job is one of the most difficult jobs we'll ever tackle and you've been successful.

You'll want to enter the new arena free from job search concerns that may have become a habit. You're no longer in a position of *asking* for an opportunity.

Now's the time to show what you can do. You'll be meeting and greeting new coworkers and getting in step with a new boss and his or her work style. It's time to switch gears and prepare to be comfortable in your new position. Most people find it easier to approach a person who appears to be easygoing and your positive mindset invites coworkers to feel comfortable with you, pronto.

Your command of business etiquette is especially valuable during this period. Now, take a deep breath and visualize yourself as one who is no longer unemployed but one who is returning to the workplace.

Perhaps you're a working mother or father who took time off from a career to care for a newborn or to rear young children.

You may be working in a job that's completely unrelated to the position you last held. With the passing of time, your life experience has molded you into a somewhat different person. The workplace has changed, too. At the least, there's an entirely new vocabulary in the pipeline and you've got to get up to speed.

If you're like many working parents, you still have responsibilities for a young family and you're the chief of operations at home. It's good to know that as you sharpen business etiquette skills that assist you to succeed in the workplace, you'll add to the arsenal of techniques that enable you to work better with people on the homefront, too.

Conversely, the winning ways you employ when you interact with housepainters, wallpaper hangers, automobile mechanics, shoe salesmen, plumbers, your children's teachers, and others will be assimilated into the courteous and persuasive methods you'll use at your new job. Accordingly, you may already have more to offer than you realize.

Today, gainful employment after retirement is not unusual.

If you're returning to the workplace after a period of retirement your personal goals are probably different than they were earlier in your employment career. You may have held an executive position and are returning to the workplace in an entirely different role. Or you may have accepted a position that you know is temporary.

If you moved to a different state before you obtained your job or you're working in a different industry, you should expect to enter a different work environment than the one you vacated. People may be more casual in your new workplace, or more formal. If, for example, you were called Mr. or Mrs. most of your working life, you may be surprised to be referred to by your first name in your new setting.

In any event, it's important to focus on the here and now.

You may not be able to rely solely upon old, tried-and-true methods of interacting with people. You'll want to be alert to current trends and attitudes and notice how people respond to your actions.

One of the benefits of returning to the workforce after retirement is that you're not likely to rust! So says an anonymous German proverb:

"*Rast ich, so rost ich.*" When I rest, I rust.

You certainly won't rust when you adapt to new and different ways in the workplace. Although adapting, learning, and growing were acceptable patterns prior to retirement, many people view retirement as a kind of earned diploma or a mark of completion. They think that adapting, learning, and growing on the job is passe. It's not!

The fact that you're reading *Everyday Business Etiquette* announces that you don't embrace that mindset. Still, the words "forewarned forearmed" from Cervantes's *Don Quixote* are worth noting.

If you've been away from the workforce due to a prolonged illness or for some other reason, welcome back! Get ready to embrace your new self image. Management has just given you a vote of confidence by hiring you and your new job title helps to describe the new you.

Anyone returning to the workforce is well served by adopting a positive attitude. A new job is cause for celebration and should put you in the proper frame of mind. You may feel as though you're on shaky ground in the early days, but if you arrive ready to accentuate the positive, you'll be off to a good start.

The queries that follow are intended to help you focus on situations you're likely to confront. If you don't feel comfortable with the solutions provided, consider other ways you can handle a challenge. This exercise will help you prepare for your return.

If you're returning to the workforce in a management or executive capacity, you'll want to peruse the following. Also read "First Days in the Manager's Chair," the second series of questions and answers in this section.

The First Few Days at a New Job

Query: Should I park my car in any space I choose even though spaces appear to be numbered and assigned?

Solution: It's discourteous to take someone's parking space and fines or penalties may result, too. The personnel department will probably provide you with parking-lot information in advance of your first day on the job but if you should face this dilemma, look around the perimeter of the lot for unmarked spaces and select one of them. Or look for a patrolling company security truck and ask the driver for instructions. If you use a parking space but you're unsure as to whether it's acceptable, ask for clarification from someone in charge at the reception desk. If that's not feasible, ask your boss.

Although it may feel awkward to ask your boss about something that seems as trivial as a parking space, it announces you're a careful and considerate individual and prefer to act correctly. That's a good message to send.

Query: If there's a van pool for people who commute to the job-site, should I ask to join?

Solution: It's probably best to wait for time to pass before you ask about joining a van pool. Give the people in the van pool some time to get to know you and there's a good chance they'll approach you with an invitation. It's possible, however, that there isn't any room for another commuter in the pool that serves your geographic area. So don't assume that coworkers are snubbing you if you don't get an offer to participate.

Query: If I'm not invited to join others at lunch time, should I ask if I can tag along?

Solution: In most cases, someone in the crowd reaches out to a new arrival and extends an invitation. Still, there may be a myriad of reasons why this doesn't occur. You may have been hired for a position that one or two of the employees coveted and sought. They may not feel kindly toward you even though that kind of response isn't logical. Moreover, other people may be aware of the intrigue and prefer to stay in the background. Accordingly, there's no one-size-fits-all solution. It may be best to dine alone for a week or two but don't wait longer than that if you'd prefer to join others. If you wait too long, you risk appearing standoffish.

Query: If coworkers are collecting money for a worthy cause but I haven't yet received my first paycheck and I'm not in a position to contribute, must I explain?

Solution: No. You may want to say something like, "I'll be ready for you next time." It's inconsiderate for anyone to press you to make a contribution especially when you've just become an employee. A vague response should work for you since you're certainly not obligated to explain further.

You may want to look at the employee handbook and check company policy regarding donations. If donations are frequently solicited, you'll want to consider whether or not you'll participate and how you will respond next time. If you set a pattern that's comfortable for you at the onset, you won't have to make excuses further down the road.

"I have two favorite charities that I support. So when I'm ready to make another donation, that's where my money goes" is the kind of statement that can set the record straight.

You'll be making many important choices in the first few days on the job and this particular challenge isn't a priority matter. Still, it's worth exploring because if you set the record straight regarding any sensitive issue, you put the challenge to rest.

Query: How will I recognize the office gossip? And how should I respond to this person?

Solution: It's true that one or more coworkers are likely to tell you a great deal about the office, the company, and other workers in an attempt to show you the ropes. The office gossip (and there may be more than one) generally likes to volunteer titillating information. A statement such as: "Hank Carter is our ace salesman, but boy does he drink his lunch" is the kind of news you hear from an office gossip. Obviously, it isn't necessary to tell you more about Carter than his status as a top salesman. You're well advised to listen without comment. As the weeks stretch on, coworkers' tendencies to gossip or speak ill of others will become apparent to you.

A gossip breaches the good judgment which is inherent to business etiquette. You have little to gain and much to lose if you consort with the office gossip. If you like to gossip, do it with your personal friends and family, and not on company time.

Query: If a procedure is explained to me but I don't understand, should I fake it?

Solution: It may not be necessary to admit you don't understand a procedure when you expect to have additional opportunities to see it demonstrated. Listen carefully. Ask questions. Remember, Rome wasn't built in a day.

On the other hand, if you know you're about to take charge and you don't completely understand what you're to do, you'd better speak up. Common courtesy demands that you don't knowingly throw a monkey wrench into the works.

Query: What should I do if I know more about the company's products or services than the coworker who is training me?

Solution: Listen carefully anyway. It's impossible to know ahead of time that there's nothing new for you to discover. If the training is slated to go on for many weeks, you may want to tell the trainer that you are ready to move ahead more quickly. Offer to explain why it is you're so well informed.

You risk offending the trainer if you yawn, stretch, slump in your chair, or otherwise demonstrate that you feel bored.

Query: Should I correct people who don't pronounce my name correctly?

Solution: Yes. Help an individual to remember your name by giving him or her an association crutch, if possible. You might say something like, "Although the family name, Powel, is spelled with a "w" it's pronounced Poel, rhymes with Joel." Do your best to remember coworkers' names and pronounce them correctly, too. Saying and spelling a person's name correctly is a basic tenet of business etiquette.

Query: My children want to call me at work when they return home from school. Do I have to notify my manager about this call, which should become a daily call?

Solution: It's probably best that your children originate the call so you don't wrongfully incur telephone expenses for the company. However, it's essential that you mention this plan to your manager and ask rather than tell your boss what you want to do. Consider, too, what your children should do if you're attending a meeting or handling company business when they call. It's unreasonable to expect company personnel to routinely take your personal messages.

First Few Days in the Manager's Chair

Query: I think it's important to listen to employees, but in these early days, I want to establish my own imprint. How much listening is necessary?

Solution: It's okay to let employees know you'll expect and appreciate their input and will actively solicit it in the near future. When you're ready to listen, listen carefully, and make it happen sooner rather than later.

Query: My administrative assistant is a man. Would he be offended if I asked him to operate my office coffeepot every morning?

Solution: Offer to share the coffee-making chores with your assistant. In this way, you shouldn't offend either a male or female assistant. There's no one-size-fits-all answer. Some assistants believe coffee-making chores aren't part of the job description. By sharing the chores, you tend to defuse what could otherwise be a touchy situation.

Query: Morale is terrible. Everyone thinks I've been brought in to downsize the department. What can I do to boost morale without divulging confidential information?

Solution: Morale suffers when worrisome rumors run rampant. Low morale is an incubator for short tempers and less than gracious behavior. Conditions may not be as bad as employees think. Call a meeting and communicate. You may be able to allay fears without getting too specific. If some employees are about to be dismissed, let everyone know that management is arranging for outplacement assistance and in some cases six-month severance pay will be awarded. If appropriate, convince your boss to sweeten the pot so productivity doesn't suffer too much.

Query: My secretary tells me she has handled heavy responsibilities for the individual I replaced. I think she's exaggerating. How should I proceed?

Solution: Give your secretary some room to spread her wings. She may want to do more than she was formerly permitted to do or she may be exaggerating. Ask for progress reports at frequent intervals. If she isn't equal to an assignment, you'll find out before any damage is done and you won't generate feelings of ill-will by questioning her ability to perform.

ON-THE-CAREER-PATH TIPS

- Read Chapter Four: Mastering Nonverbal Communication
- Read Chapter Five: Courteous Behavior with Members of the Opposite Sex
- Read Chapter Ten: Introductions

STRATEGY YOU CAN USE

Here's how early days at a new job compare to trial by jury:

(1) You sit in the jury box and try not to make judgments until you've heard all the arguments.

It's a good strategy to adapt when you're returning to the workplace after a long hiatus because, unlike someone who is completely new to the workplace, you probably have expectations based upon past work experiences. The tendency to compare your new job to a former job or your new boss's management style to another boss's management style is natural but largely unproductive.

(2) At the same time, you're on trial. New coworkers don't know you or what to expect from you.

In a nutshell:

- Don't make judgments about others.
- Do expect others to make judgments about you.

Or, as Will Shakespeare's Hamlet said: "Give every man thy ear, but few thy voice; Take each man's censure, but reserve thy judgment."

When you do, you'll court everyone's approval and you won't take umbrage if others act standoffish.

As the early days fade and weeks escalate to months, you'll accumulate the information necessary to bring in a verdict. So, too, will coworkers.

Don't be surprised if, when you need computer operation instructions, the most helpful individual is the one who appeared to be the most inaccessible in your early days on the job.

Don't be surprised if the courteous behavior you display to the young man in the mailroom is remembered long after when that young man moves into a top managerial position and tends to favor your requests.

Such things happen all the time.

WHEN YOU'RE PROMOTED OR HAVE A NEW JOB WITHIN THE COMPANY

Congratulations! You're likely to hear that praise often as you take on new responsibilities in your company.

Many people find they're uncomfortable accepting praise. They probably don't stop to think how a brusque response makes the individual who extends the good wishes feel foolish.

Take the time to graciously acknowledge all expressions of goodwill no matter how often you hear them and no matter whether or not you think they're sincere.

Some promotions are accompanied by printed formal announcements and you may receive written notes of congratulations from those who receive the announcements. It's good form and it makes good business sense to tell the message sender you appreciate his or her sentiments. This doesn't mean you must write a note, too. It does suggest, however, that you say thank you the very next time you communicate with the individual.

When you correspond, add a line or two to acknowledge receipt of the congratulatory greeting. If you telephone the individual to discuss business, don't end the conversation until you say thank you.

"Bill, I appreciated your note. You always find time to offer kind words when anyone enjoys some success. That's an admirable quality. Thanks again."

Public Relations

It may be appropriate for you to generate publicity regarding your new position if your company doesn't take the initiative to do so. Aside from feeling good about your achievement and wanting to shout out the news, the opportunity to indulge in personal advertising can generate sales opportunities and earn speaking engagements or invitations to participate in some advantageous capacity in community or trade-association events.

If you initiate a press release for newspapers or a trade association publication, don't hesitate to toot your own horn. Remember, however, that a published press release amounts to a free advertisement. The publication's editor will probably be more inclined to print your release if it isn't overly self-serving. If, for example, your new position came about as a result of company reengineering and your company is a leader in its field, the new, streamlined operation may be considered newsworthy and your new position will be touted along with this information. Of course, you wouldn't want to act as a company spokesperson without proper authority to do so, but a published announcement can be valuable and engineering it can be worth your time and effort.

Plan to send copies of published announcements to customers, clients, suppliers, and colleagues in your industry. There's power in the printed word!

Look the Part

It's not likely you received your promotion or your new position if you didn't look as though you belonged in the new environment. Nevertheless, your staff and others will be scrutinizing you carefully in the early days and weeks and your attention to grooming and wardrobe is important. Your personal appearance should lend support to your authority.

Don't allow the added hours or concentration you devote to new responsibilities prevent you from maintaining your standards. Take time for a haircut. Be attentive to your garments' dry cleaning or tailoring requirements. You may want to shop for new accessories (i.e., ties, scarves, braces, stockings) which can add interest and variety to your wardrobe. It's not unusual to feel stressed when you're working hard to adjust to your new role. New accessories may help to decorate your spirits as well as your appearance. When you feel good about yourself, you're more inclined to smile and practice your best manners!

Leadership

You may no longer be a coworker but instead you're the boss. Your new position can put a strain on relationships and you'll want to do your best to minimize misunderstandings. Consider the words of the ancient Chinese philosopher Lao-tzu:

> *"I have three treasures. Guard and keep them:*
> *The first is deep love,*
> *The second is frugality,*
> *And the third is not to dare to be ahead of the world.*
> *Because of deep love, one is courageous.*
> *Because of frugality, one is generous.*
> *Because of not daring to be ahead of the world, one becomes the leader of the world."*

Everyday Business Etiquette is not devoted to the subject of leadership. Still, when you're promoted or in a new position within your company, you're likely to find yourself in a leadership position. Your mastery and use of business etiquette can pave the way for a productive transition.

The advice of Lao-tzu is not to be ahead of the world. If you accept this philosophy you'll listen carefully to everyone, smile and acknowledge others, invite feedback, know how and when to offer praise, and take your new position seriously while not taking yourself too seriously.

If you don't accept this philosophy, these are still appropriate behavior patterns and should enhance your performance in your new position.

Rites of passage

Will you park your car in the same parking lot?

Will you eat your lunch with the same people?

Do you have keys to the executive washroom?

Do you have clearance to access expanded computer data?

Subtle alterations are part and parcel of most new positions. Some are perquisites, others are necessary to support job performance.

Former colleagues may expect to be favored and share in your rewards. They may be dismayed if you no longer spend time with them to indulge in small talk. The old green-eyed monster, jealousy, can be at work. They may agree among themselves that you're standoffish, uncooperative, or too big for your boots!

If that happens, you're likely to get a cool reception when you approach them and if you expect their full cooperation in the workplace, you're probably going to be disappointed.

Professionally speaking, you'll want to be on reasonable terms with everyone. When you express enthusiasm about your new position, take care not to help fan a fire. There's sometimes a fine line between expressing enthusiasm and being boastful.

A statement such as "The executive dining room menu is terrific and makes it easy for me to stick to my low-fat diet" can be interpreted to mean "She doesn't eat with the peons anymore and thinks she's better than we are."

Of course, you can't control someone's mean-spirited response to your success, but you can be sensitive to the ruffled-feathers syndrome. It's a case of feeling left out and unappreciated, and it can lead to sulking.

This is probably a good time for you to listen more, talk less and gradually eliminate some practices, rather than make abrupt changes. Perhaps you'll take a coffee break with a former coworker if you don't join him for lunch.

Actions that convey an "I miss you" message should be appreciated. In fact, when you demonstrate that others aren't forgotten or unappreciated, you win supporters.

While former colleagues know you well, new ones don't. They may be wary. Moreover, they may be ready to judge you against the person you replaced. If that individual was widely admired, a mentor to others, and extremely popular, you have a hard act to follow.

As you work to establish your own hallmark, remember that you're the new kid on the block and you'll have to give people time to get to know you.

Some of tactics you use with former coworkers should work well with new colleagues, too. Listen more, talk less. Demonstrate that you enjoy their company by being ready to join them for lunch or coffee breaks.

Since you can't be in two places at once, you'll have to determine priorities. While you juggle your schedule and try to please everyone, take comfort in the knowledge that rites of passage are short lived.

Once you comprehend how others are impacted by your move, you'll be in an excellent position to calm fears and soothe concerns. In addition, you'll lay a firm foundation upon which to grow and excel in your new role with the company.

ON-THE-CAREER-PATH TIPS

- Read Chapter Seven: Send a Message with Your Wardrobe Selections
- Read Chapter Four: Mastering Nonverbal Communication

INSIGHT YOU CAN USE (Not exactly a strategy)

Patience Is a Virtue "Strategy." When people tell you something, they inevitably show you something, too.

- Tell: "I can't meet the deadline."
  Show: An unhappy individual who may feel overwhelmed.
- Tell: "I've got to ask my boss."
  Show: Someone who probably doesn't have authority to act.
- Tell: "You're too sensitive."
  Show: A person who may regret her words or deeds.
- Tell: "I'll get the job done."
  Show: A confident employee.

Of course, these illustrations are tentative because they *stand alone.* When someone you know tells you something, you generally have more background information. For example:

"I can't meet the deadline."

You know this individual hasn't cooperated since he was transferred to your department. You know he has the skills to get the job done. You know he has sufficient time to meet the deadline. You also suspect he may be depressed owing to personal problems you've heard him discuss.

His failure to meet this deadline shows you it's time for you to act on the bigger problem and not simply extend the deadline or assign someone else to work on the project.

"You're too sensitive."

You've had earlier demonstrations of this person's tactless behavior. You've seen two of your coworkers turn on their heels and look flustered as they hurried away from him. He has told you that you're too sensitive more than once.

His comments show you it's time to confront him about his unacceptable behavior, or to seek advice about him from someone whose judgment you respect.

People often proceed differently when they have more information. Information gathering takes time. Since most folks want everything accomplished yesterday, it's easy to recognize that patience is indeed a virtue.

When you're in a new position in your company, you stand alone. Help others to know you better as fast as possible. Here's how the practice of good business etiquette can help you get the job done:

- Be accurate and attentive when you take and deliver a telephone message to a colleague and you show you're *trustworthy.*
- If someone is working long hours to complete an assignment, bring a cup of coffee or container of juice to his desk and you'll demonstrate that you're *considerate.*
- When a meeting planner is stymied because the slide projector won't operate, offer to obtain another one from the next department and you'll show you're *cooperative.*
- If a client arrives to meet your boss and puts his soggy raincoat on the upholstered reception room chair, tell the client you'll take care of his raincoat for him. Whisk it away to where you can hang it to dry. You'll *demonstrate your respect for company property.* Moreover, you'll make the client feel pampered, and that can't hurt.
- When a coworker is away because of a death in the family, send a condolence note. You don't have to know someone for a long time to recognize the pain following the loss of a loved one. Send a simple message and you'll demonstrate you're a *caring individual who displays good judgment.*

If others in your office pay a condolence call, you may want to join them. This courtesy call announces to coworkers that you're *one of their group.* Don't plan to pay a condolence call alone, however, if you've just moved into the new position. You don't want to appear to be pushy.

- When a coworker makes a presentation to a gathering, take a private moment to say something complimentary.

"I liked the slide program you assembled. It was very clever. Nice job." Or, "I was impressed with they way you handled the question-and-answer session. You really know your subject. Now I know more about it, too. Thanks."

Your acknowledgement of another person's good job is a *likeable quality.* Many people forget that even the most seasoned speaker can have self-doubts. Your confirmation of a job well done will be fondly remembered.

WHEN YOU ACCEPT A JOB WITH A DIFFERENT COMPANY

When you accept a job with a different company you'll probably find yourself making comparisons. Rule number one:

Don't complain. These are the kind of comments to avoid:

"Telephone service was more efficient at Company A. I have to share a telephone with coworkers and I don't like the electronic voice-mail message options."

"I liked being a team-member at Company A. Here, team-members don't have much power. At least, I don't have much power. I've got to report to my manager daily and explain myself to obtain clearance to access special records. How will I be able to meet deadlines?"

Remember what your mother told you: "If you can't say something nice, don't say anything."

Moreover, the tendency to find things that are wrong with the new company can become a bad habit. You're well advised to focus on what you like about your new position. It will help you to feel good about what you're doing. When you feel good, it's easier to make others feel good, too.

You'll establish a comfort zone in which to operate. When coworkers, customers, and management people approach you in that climate, there's an ease and grace to communications. Business can be conducted smoothly.

As William Shakespeare wrote in *Much Ado About Nothing,* ". . . comparisons are odious."

Instead of making comparisons, use your observations to stimulate positive actions. If, for example, the telephone system at your new job has drawbacks, jot down what you observe and keep the focus on cause and effect:

"A caller must listen to too many options to access voice-mail to leave a message. Half my callers begin their messages with the word, 'Finally.' In an attempt to be efficient, are we irritating callers and perhaps losing business?"

"I can't act on much without approval from my manager. When she's in a meeting, or unavailable, I have waited for a day or more to get her approval. Is she planning to empower me to act on my own after an initial trial period? At the moment, I risk meeting project deadlines."

Confront your boss or the appropriate executive with specific concerns. When you focus on the good of the company and your ability to sharpen your performance, you should inspire useful feedback.

In this way, the know-how you bring to your new job can be used to promote positive changes in your new company. On the chance that nothing comes from your efforts, don't allow disappointment to cramp your style. Several things may occur:

- Change will come but it will take time
- A new boss or new management may come on board and make positive changes
- You may move into a position of authority which enables you to make changes

If your list is long, however, you may decide you don't want to work for this company longer than necessary. In that case, your efforts to maintain composure under adverse conditions and display impeccable business etiquette will reap two benefits. One, you will prove to yourself that you're skilled and capable when conditions are adverse. (Take a bow!) Two, you're not likely to generate feelings of ill-will and therefore, you should receive a good reference from this employer when you leave.

On the other hand, don't make disparaging remarks about your former company in an effort to please your new boss or coworkers. When people listen to someone making negative remarks about others they often wonder what negative comments that person will make about them, given the opportunity.

Your commitment to confidentiality and ethical behavior can be called into question if comments about your former company or boss appear to be in poor taste. Moreover, you may have signed a confidentiality agreement for your former employer. If so, it's wise to make sure you understand its terms and comply with them.

Take your experience, your skills, and your know-how to this new position in a different company but expect to tailor them to fit needs. If the company's business is manufacturing and you formerly toiled in a service industry, similarities are likely to be few and far between.

New Town?

If you moved to a new location to work for this company, you must acquaint yourself with a new living environment, too. Give priority to learning about the goods and services that support you at work. Your real-estate agent, local chamber of commerce, or the company's personnel office may have newcomer information literature you can rely upon for recommendations concerning:

- Child-care services
- Private schools
- Driver's license and registration offices and hours
- Modes of transportation
- Radio stations that announce local road conditions
- Dry cleaners
- Hair-care services
- Clothing boutiques

Arm yourself with information you need to arrive at your workplace on time, well dressed and groomed, and ready to devote yourself to your work. If you have a youngster or older parent in your charge, you'll want to make necessary arrangements for this relative's care and well-being when you're away from home.

It breaches the boundaries of business etiquette when you're in a new position at a new company and receive numerous personal calls, are tardy in arriving, make special requests to leave early, or are absent from the job.

It's What You Know That Counts

You may have learned about the company you're now working for prior to your job interview or you may have seen a training film that introduced the company to you. In any event, the more you know about your new company the better prepared you'll be to perform.

When a customer asks questions, you'll give accurate information. Moreover, you won't risk sending a customer away because you didn't realize your company performs a service the customer requires.

You won't often rely upon coworkers to assist you, demonstrating that you're willing and able to pull your share of the load. This helps cement a healthy relationship with the people with whom you now work.

When you're new in the company, introductions are made but your deeds really announce who you are. Do ask questions when you don't have the answers. Not only will you provide customers with appropriate information, you'll learn. Your behavior will demonstrate that you're not a know-it-all.

Take care to learn the names of people and their positions within the company. It's the kind of information that should prevent you from making a serious faux pas. You don't want to go over someone's head and consult with his or her boss when, in fact, the company's organizational chart points to a consultation at a lower level. Your understanding of in-house hierarchy will demonstrate your respect for good form.

Taking Sides

What you know about the alliances between coworkers is important, too. If two factions conflict, each one is likely to woo you to join their camp. It's generally accepted that might makes right. If you resist joining either group you risk inviting ire from both camps. If you're sympathetic to one group's reasoning, you risk alienating others. It's a no-win situation.

Let the tenets of business etiquette be your guide and you'll find it easier to stay clear of coworkers' intrigues.

Listen carefully.

Joe complained about Ben's management style to Hank who had worked in the department for about two weeks. "He came back from a six-week training program and he thinks he knows everything." Hank knew that Joe was waiting for him to comment but he remained silent.

A few days later, Ben approached Hank and told him not to feel hampered by Joe's old fashioned way of working. "He doesn't like computers. Wants to see every little detail down on paper." Hank didn't say a word.

Four weeks later, Joe was chosen to attend the company's six-week training program. When he returned to the office, he and Ben talked about the program and decided they could work together to make positive changes. Hank guessed that if he had said anything negative about either Ben or Joe earlier, he'd probably be out of favor with both of them by now.

Be courteous to everyone.

A group of coworkers went to lunch together but George wasn't in a hurry to finish his meal. Sally, who had recently joined the company, didn't want to be late but didn't want to leave George alone at the table when the others left. They were both about fifteen minutes late returning to the office. Two days later, Sally purposely arrived at the office fifteen minutes early. She noticed that George was already at his desk. When she came in early another day George was there, too. She was pleased with herself for staying with George until he finished his lunch. Apparently he wasn't a laggard, and although it was a small courtesy, she felt it was an important one. Surely her sense of what was proper didn't go unnoticed by George or the others at lunch that day. She probably earned their respect. You can't know in advance the effect of every action you take, but when you do something because you believe it to be proper, it should work to your advantage.

Don't prejudge anyone based upon what you've heard from others.

Marge was told that Dale didn't see well enough to get a driver's license. As a result, Marge assumed Dale didn't see her unless they were standing near to one another. When Marge was more than five feet away from Dale she didn't make any attempt to greet her or to make eye contact. Dale thought that Marge was standoffish and began to avoid her. Later, Dale was promoted to division manager and automatically excluded Marge from her list of candidates for an assistant.

Think before you speak.

Everyone could tell from the photograph on Pat's desk that her young sister was wheelchair bound. Naturally, Pat was especially sensitive to the needs of handicapped people. When Pat confronted her new assistant, Ned, about his tardiness, he blamed his problem on the increased number of handicapped parking spaces the company assigned to the parking lot he used. "What about my rights?" he asked. "Doesn't a normal person deserve as much consideration as a cripple?"

Ned didn't endear himself to Pat with these comments. She wasn't likely to forget about his insensitivity toward the handicapped. Ned's thoughtless comments helped install a permanent barricade between himself and his new boss.

ON-THE-CAREER-PATH TIPS

- Read Chapter Four: Mastering Nonverbal Communication
- Read Chapter Seven: Send a Message with Your Wardrobe Selections
- Read Chapter Ten: Introductions

STRATEGY YOU CAN USE

Remember the enthusiasm you felt when you were first hired? Take it to the workplace!

It's not unusual to fell a little unsure of yourself when you start to work for a new company but why let others know?

Act with enthusiasm, vigor, zest, eagerness. Those good vibrations you emit will camouflage any hesitancy or skepticism you may harbor and your exuberance and positive attitude will show others that you hold them in high esteem. If you're so happy to join them, they must be doing something right!

An enthusiasm-to-the-rescue strategy is useful any time you're a little unsure of yourself. Take notice of the affect this strategy has on you, too. In effect, you treat yourself to a pep talk and raise your level of performance.

TRAVELING TO DISTANT PLACES TO CONDUCT BUSINESS

It's not unusual to feel ill at ease when you find yourself in new and different surroundings.

You can't find the gas-cap release on the rented car, you didn't know that Main becomes a one-way street after 4:30 P.M., and you can't be sure when the airlines will deliver your lost luggage to the hotel. If you were at home you'd be driving your own car, have no need to traverse Main Street, and you'd know exactly where to find your clean socks.

If you're one of those folks who becomes tense and tight-lipped or short-tempered under these conditions, pause and reflect. Your personal comfort level can affect your performance and since you're here to conduct business, compose yourself!

> *"Great events make me quiet and calm; it is only trifles that irritate my nerves."*
>
> Victoria, queen of England (Letter to King Leopold of Belgium, 1848)

Remember these annoyances are trifles and the great event is the business ahead. Focus on that and you'll be more likely to put your best foot forward rather than put your foot in your mouth!

Seven Courteous Responses to Irritating "Trifles"

(1) When your flight is delayed, heavy traffic detains you or a car breaks down, find a telephone as soon as possible and contact anyone who is waiting to meet you, or is otherwise inconvenienced by your delay. Although you'd prefer to concentrate on getting yourself back on track, you must take the time to be considerate to others.

(2) If you're traveling with a colleague who is a person of the opposite sex and the hotel reservations were mistakenly made for Mr. and Mrs., act to straighten the error out immediately, in a good-humored manner. Your easy style will minimize embarrassment and confusion. It will be appreciated by your colleague who, no doubt, is tired and anxious to settle into his or her room. Even though business men and women frequently travel together, a hint that someone is a clandestine sexual partner, rather than a business associate, leads to further misunderstandings. Lock the barn door before the horse runs away!

(3) Will a woman offend her male business associate if she drives the car, reaches for and pays restaurant bills, or carries her own luggage? It's another no one-size-answer-fits-all question. You demonstrate sensitivity and good form when you carefully observe how your male colleague responds to your command of an occasion. If you're truly secure in your position, permitting or expecting your male associate to assume the traditional "man's role" is desirable. If the company isn't responsible for some expenses, tally costs and reimburse your share without delay, although not necessarily in view of waiters and other service providers.

If, however, you want to inject some balance into proceedings, do so with grace. As you walk towards the driver's side of the car say, "I'd really like to drive, John. I know this part of town quite well."

(4) You're directed to a seat near the restaurant's kitchen door and the dining room is crowded. You arrived about ten minutes early and your host wasn't there. Nevertheless, you gave the head waiter a gratuity and arranged for another table. When your host arrives, he presses $20.00 into your hand, saying that he saw as he came in that you made arrangements for a better table. You feel foolish. Moreover, you gave the waiter $10.00. Although this isn't exactly a universal challenge, it represents various sticky situations you're likely to confront when you socialize with people you hardly know while in the process of conducting business. Let the matter drop. If you don't, you risk making "the other guy" feel foolish. It's not worth the risk.

(5) If someone consumes too many alcoholic beverages, don't permit the individual to drive. Even if you believe you may risk offending the individual,

don't shrink from intervening. You may associate wine or strong spirits with relaxation, and the opportunity to "have a few" may be inviting. Remember your system may react differently in this new environment (e.g., hot weather, high altitude, different time zone) and you may not be able to consume your usual number of drinks without ill effect. Don't be the one who others won't allow to drive. You'll embarrass yourself and your company. Moreover, you jeopardize business goals when you demonstrate loss of control.

(6) Don't forget your colleagues back at the office. If your business trip takes you to an exotic location, you may want to return to the office with an indigenous treat for staff members who assumed duties you would normally handle. It's a small courtesy, helps you to say thank you, and generates goodwill.

How does this topic qualify as an annoyance? It can become a problem if you forget to include someone who should be included. Don't forget.

One gift everyone back at the office may enjoy is a photograph album filled with photographs you take during the trip or with picture postcards or slides you purchase at local gift shops, or all three. If, for example, you travel to Alaska to visit a major customer, the folks back at the office will learn more about this customer based upon your "gift."

(7) The casual atmosphere during sightseeing excursions, long waits at an airport, or a cab ride back to the hotel late at night following a business gathering, may lure a colleague, client, or customer into saying something indiscreet. The result? In an effort to later distance himself or herself from the unfortunate remarks, the person distances himself or herself from you. Accordingly, this is one time it's polite to interrupt someone who is talking! Change the subject. Also, avoid making statements you yourself may come to regret.

Promote Yourself

When you travel to distant places to conduct business, consider yourself a goodwill ambassador. You'll promote yourself in two different ways.

First, when you promote yourself to the position of goodwill ambassador, you'll focus only on saying things that flatter your local contacts or, at the least, don't offend them. If, for example, you hail from sunny Tucson and you're in Manhattan during February's bone-chilling cold weather, you won't ask, "How can you stand this awful weather?" If you're from Manhattan and visiting Tucson in February, you'll talk about the lovely weather instead of saying, "The food is so highly seasoned, how can you eat it?"

Second, promote yourself and your company by demonstrating your concern for others. Be a good listener. Speak well of your colleagues and workplace and accentuate similarities. This works well even when you're all employed by the same company. If you're working in distant places, you have been little more than names and extension numbers to one another. This in-person contact helps to put a face on people who make up the company.

It's a perfect opportunity to increase your network of contacts. If you find, for example, the administrative assistant who supports the person you're visiting is especially helpful, ask if you may contact her for assistance at a later date. It's a gracious way to praise the skill she demonstrated. Invite her to call on you if you can ever be of service. Leave your business card with her and, if appropriate, tell her more about your job so she'll know how you may assist her and her boss.

On Your Return

When you return to your office, your boss will probably appreciate an oral report, though it's not required. Open communications help build trust, and since we tend to favor people we trust, your comments should have a positive affect.

Does someone deserve a thank-you note?

If you received royal treatment from someone with whom you visited, a short, handwritten note should be sent immediately upon your return to the office. The fact that you already said thank you doesn't excuse you from sending a note. Keep it short and simple and refer to specific highlights:

"It's not an exaggeration to say that my life has been enriched by the steamboat ride on the Mississippi. I have you to thank for insisting that I not miss this golden opportunity and for taking the time to accompany me, as well."

"I thought I'd eaten some fine Mexican food in my time but the dinner you arranged for me and my colleagues to enjoy at El Charro was exceptional.

While you're writing thank-you notes, don't neglect to thank people in your home office who assumed some of your duties while you were away or were helpful to you in preparing for the trip.

If communications at your location routinely speed along via electronic mail, you can use this forum to send your message. You're never incorrect, however, when you opt to send a personal, handwritten note of thanks to someone. Do so without delay or the message will lose its luster.

ON-THE-CAREER-PATH TIPS

- Read Chapter Three: Dining-Table Etiquette You Didn't Learn at Home
- Read Chapter Eleven: Gratuities
- Read Chapter Twelve: Correspondence

People can't display impeccable manners when they're under extreme stress. If you or someone you know fears flying but is required to fly to distant places to conduct business, be aware that help is available.

The Pegasus Fear of Flying Foundation conducts nine-hour seminars at airports and corporate training facilities [(800) 332-7668]. It's one of several programs in the marketplace. Expect to pay $350.00 or more for this kind of assistance. If flight is an ordeal, you may think the price is of small consequence.

On or about October 1, 1996, Pegasus will release a package consisting of a one-hour video, two-hour take-along audio tape, and thirty-minute relaxation tape, as well as a textbook and guide, and a toll-free number to call for advice. Projected cost is $49.95 plus postage.

Books, tapes, and other sources of professional help are available, too. Check with customer-service representatives at your local airport or ask your travel agent for information about other programs and materials aimed at people who suffer from aerophobia.

STRATEGY YOU CAN USE

Keep your eye on the big picture but at the same time don't minimize the importance of details.

- It's a balancing act. You're a juggler. The good news is you only need do one thing at one time. So focus on what's needed when it's needed and be assured you'll attend to details when the time is right. Many people feel stress when they must work in a new and different environment and this approach enables you to avoid feeling overwhelmed.

- Part of the big picture of life is enjoyment. A trip to a different place can be personally enriching. Don't get so bogged down with business and details that you forget to have a good time. Moreover, your genuine interest in new people and new places translates into enthusiasm and approval and those attributes compliment the people you have come to see.

WHEN CONVENTION TIME IS JUST AROUND THE CORNER

If you're going to represent your firm at the company booth or display on the convention floor, you'll want to be poised for success! Poise (grace, style, and refinement) is basic to *Everyday Business Etiquette.*

- Your smile and handshake should be in top working condition. You're acting as a greeter and naturally you want to make people feel welcome. If it's impractical to shake hands with the large numbers who assemble, a pleasant appearance and winning ways will suffice. A smile cuts across any language barrier and tells a person you are glad he or she is present.

If you maintain a mustache or whiskers, be mindful of how your grooming practices affect your smile. If you experiment with different lip colors, be sure your convention-day selection enhances your smile. Make necessary adjustments or decisions before convention days arrive.

When it comes to a handshake, a cool, firm handshake is businesslike and appropriate. If your palms tend to be sweaty, you may want to keep an absorbent handkerchief in your pocket so that you can dry your palms as necessary.

- A convention floor often has a carnival-like atmosphere and this energy may help you to sustain your own high energy level. When you're enthusiastic and up-beat, you transmit the message that something exciting is happening. Your body language (e.g., standing, smiling, making eye contact) helps send a positive message to others and invites them to get involved.

Don't permit the time demands of the occasion to rob you of required sleep or make you forget good eating habits. Candy bars instead of a good lunch will affect your performance. It's possible to make better choices for yourself if you plan ahead.

If you're sharing a platform with coworkers, it's likely you'll indulge in a gabfest when time permits. Make certain that a convention attendee arriving at the booth is not kept waiting because you're chatting. The convention serves business purposes. It's rude to make someone wait to conduct business while you're involved in a personal conversation. Your coworker should excuse you if you interrupt to take care of the public, and vice versa.

It's nice to make every person feel important and feel as though you're doing everything possible to provide good service. Still, when you're dealing with large numbers of people, don't make a promise you can't keep. Not only would that be a breach of trust, it could open up a can of worms.

If, for example, someone wants you to hold admission tickets for his colleague who hasn't yet arrived, it's unwise to accept the tickets. You can't guarantee their safekeeping in this setting. Moreover, even a memory expert may have difficulty remembering which face belongs to which request. You provide the best service when you do what you can do well and don't do what you can't do well!

By giving this possibility some forethought, you'll act appropriately when things are hectic and someone makes a special request. Don't be afraid to say no.

If you ask someone to sign a form, be businesslike and specific. Say, "Please sign on this line," not "Please, sign this for me." Both requests sound polite but the second one is fluff. They're not signing for you. Mean what you say and say what you mean. Although this sage advice isn't for convention time only, preconvention days are an excellent time to think about what you do and say.

People will make snap judgments about you and your company. It's the nature of the convention setting. Either they'll stay to gather more information or move on and spend precious time with your competitor. Something as subtle as an accurately worded request may boost your chances to reach company goals.

If you're stepping in to work at the company's booth in order to relieve a coworker, arrive on time. Though you'll represent the company for only a few hours, make sure you're well informed. If you're the person who is being relieved, take care to return to your post promptly. It's easy to be sidetracked in this sea of activity. When you keep someone waiting, they may keep someone waiting and you inadvertently start a chain reaction. It's not an accomplishment you wish to claim as your own!

Around the Convention Center

Trade shows and convention gatherings are typically sprawling affairs. As a result, you may see or be seen by business contacts in restaurants, at newspaper stands, or while waiting for the arrival of a local bus, as well as in hospitality suites and places where you'd expect to mingle with these folks. In short, you're in a fishbowl setting. Keep that in mind as you navigate through both work and leisure hours. Not only will you want to be mindful of your personal appearance, you'll want your good manners to show.

Stow that angry remark when coffee-shop waiting lines are long or service is slow. You shouldn't necessarily grin and bear it, but your position doesn't improve if you grimace and growl. Circumvent waits through good planning. At a busy hotel, make advance reservations or order a room-service meal.

One senior business executive claims, "You can often learn more about your playing partner in one round of golf than you can in a month of meetings."

Remember, your character shows when you participate in competitive sporting events. These days, planned exercise is common for convention or special-meeting attendees. You may find yourself delightfully engaged in some athletic competition. Be a good sport!

If you and a love interest will attend a convention together in some romantic location, it may be difficult to avoid open displays of affection, especially when the moon is full, the music is sweet, and you've just been "wined and dined." If you happen to be scantily clad as you lounge around the swimming pool, or pressed close while dancing under the stars, it may take a superhuman effort to avoid being carried away by the magic of the moment.

It's much easier to decide in advance how you'll handle romance before convention time. If you decide to maintain your professional stature and business image at all costs, you'll make it a point to avoid compromising positions.

When You're on Stage

You may serve as a panel member when a discussion group convenes, make a brief presentation to a small group of convention-goers, or address a large audience in the main ballroom. Of course, the preparation time involved will be directly related to your on-stage demands.

Let's assume, however, that you're going to serve as a member of a panel and will answer questions from the audience. If other panel members disagree with your position or members of the audience are less than friendly to your position, how will you respond?

Assess your goals when you accept the invitation to serve on the panel and make plans that permit you to achieve them. If you recognize that you're likely to be navigating shark-infested waters, decide in advance that you're going to maintain your composure. Even if you respond aggressively, you'll be tactful.

Another panel member waves a sheaf of papers and cries out that you're working with dated figures.

You assure the audience that your figures are from The ABC Survey Group and are stamped with a recent date. You rise and demand that the sheaf of papers be handed over for your examination. If the figures are from a bona fide source and differ from the figures you quoted, you can recommend that further research be initiated, or you can speak in support of ABC Survey Group's admirable track record in providing accurate and current data.

You may pound the table gently, you may wave papers in the air, you may stand up while others remain seated, and you may permit your voice level to rise an octave. You should, however, refrain from making a personal attack on your opponent. Attack the message, not the messenger. Let others draw their own conclusions. If you do this without surrendering your "cool," onlookers are likely to draw favorable conclusions about you.

If your goal as a panel participant is to showcase your know-how, advertise your company's product or service, or win converts to your point of view, remember, honey is preferable to vinegar.

Personal Space

Conventions draw people from diverse locations and it's good to remind yourself that some business etiquette rules apply even though they don't prevail in your usual business environment:

Respect a person's personal space. Kathleen Greer, president of a Massachusetts-based human resources consulting firm, advises, "Stay a bent arm away" in an article entitled "How to Mix Business with Pleasure" in the August 1995 issue of *Sales & Marketing Management.* She claims this is an acceptable distance between people in this country.

Her observation serves to underscore the point that we don't all play by the same set of rules. If someone crowds you or appears to be standoffish, he or she may be accustomed to different personal-space requirements. Factor this information into your treatment of individuals and courteously provide others with a little more than elbow room when you approach.

Some people use four-letter words as a matter of course. Their colleagues do the same and no one thinks it out of place. Others are offended by such language. They don't believe it belongs in mixed company and feel expletives are best when deleted in any company. An *Everyday Business Etiquette* recommendation? Banish swearwords or obscenities from all business conversations. They detract from your professionalism.

Convention floors are not quiet places. Neighboring restaurants and hospitality suites bustle with activity. You may find it's too much of a good thing. Find a quiet spot and permit yourself a moment or two of peaceful contemplation. Perhaps you'd enjoy having a quiet talk with yourself. Some folks claim this strategy helps them rediscover their centers. You'll enjoy the convention experience more if you don't permit loud noises and other distractions to rob you of inner peace. When you return to the throngs you'll feel refreshed, ready, and able to put your best foot forward.

ON-THE-CAREER-PATH TIPS

- Read Chapter One: When You're Away from the Office with Your Boss
- Read Chapter One: Traveling to Distant Places to Conduct Business
- Read Chapter Four: Mastering Nonverbal Communication
- Read Chapter Six: At-the-Podium Protocol

Plan to have an ample supply of business cards with you. If an area code has changed or you've been promoted, the card should indicate up-to-date data. A pen-scribbled change on the card isn't acceptable. If you're not pleased with your business card's message or appearance, the upcoming convention provides a good incentive for obtaining new cards.

STRATEGY YOU CAN USE

A convention typically showcases a multitude of goods and services that are intended to help convention attendees attain business goals.

Pack two hats when you go, your specialist's hat and your generalist's hat. You'll automatically be more receptive to broad-based information and not gravitate to goods and services that relate only to your area of expertise. Mingle with people who make varied contributions to your industry and be prepared to learn from them. If you're open to the entire convention experience, you'll find it much more enriching.

By utilizing *Everyday Business Etiquette* methods and insight, you'll navigate through the crowds with style and grace and make a favorable impact on everyone you encounter.

SPRUCING UP FOR IMPORTANT SEMINAR ATTENDANCE

One of the first things most seminar attendees receive is a name tag. It serves to remind you that you're not an anonymous member of this business crowd. Your participation will be noted by others. If you're attending an on-site seminar at your company, you'll probably mingle with coworkers from other departments whom you rarely, if ever, see. If you're attending a seminar at a hotel or resort in your town, you may be rubbing shoulders with people who are clients, customers, or potential employers. Make no mistake about it, seminar time is not time for rest and relaxation. You're in the business arena and you're well advised to act accordingly.

Your first stop is the seminar registration desk where you'll check in and obtain the name tag and specialized materials. If your boss gave you a confirmation number or you received an admission ticket, be prepared to give it to the seminar representative. If you must fumble through your briefcase or handbag to locate an admission ticket, you keep others waiting, which is not considerate and won't win you admirers.

Plan to arrive on time, too. Arriving late may mean that no one is waiting behind you to register but it also means that you'll be entering a program already in progress. Although you enter the room quietly and find an empty seat quickly, you can't help but disturb the proceedings.

If you arrive early and you know you'll have to step out of the room from time to time to call the office, or you must leave early, you may want to select a chair near an exit. If you're attending the seminar with people you know, you may want to suggest that all of you sit apart from one another. Not only will you all have an opportunity to mingle with people you don't know, you won't be tempted to engage in conversation while the speaker is talking. The speaker and members of the audience won't appreciate the distracting "buzz," and you don't want to be rude.

It's not uncommon for trainers to ask people who are seated near to one another to form small groups to conduct a learning exercise. By sitting next to people you don't know, you're likely to benefit from hearing new and different viewpoints. It's another good reason to sit apart from coworkers or acquaintances.

Be aware that short program breaks are common. They provide the chance to make telephone calls. If you rise and exit the room while the trainer is speaking, you cause a disruption. It's polite to avoid coming or going while the program is in progress so as not to disturb anyone. Moreover, you don't want to miss important information.

Make Yourself Comfortable

It's difficult to please everyone where an optimum room temperature is concerned. As a result, you may find a seminar meeting room too hot or too cold.

Don't hesitate to ask the seminar representative to arrange with the facility operator to adjust temperatures. This individual is on location to assist you and other seminar customers and should do everything possible to help make the day pleasant as well as productive.

Nevertheless, you're well advised to adopt the layer-method of dressing for a seminar. Bring a jacket or sweater you can wear if you feel cold or remove if you feel hot. Perform a top-to-toe checkup to assure that you'll be comfortably attired so that you're better able to concentrate on the presentation and maintain your good mood. It's not easy to be attentive and friendly when you're turning blue!

Speaking of friendly, most seminar trainers are precisely that. It's easy to approach them with your questions or comments and, although you may be encouraged to do so while the seminar is in progress, don't assume you can't approach the trainer privately for information, too. Of course, if seminar attendance is in the hundreds, the trainer may not be able to accommodate you. Once you realize that it's appropriate to seek out the trainer for one-on-one time together, you may feel inclined to do so and gain something valuable from the exchange.

Another Layer

In addition to toting a sweater or jacket, plan to carry your business cards. Many folks arrive at a seminar with a let's-take-time-off attitude, or a this-learning-experience-is-a-treat-for-me philosophy. In either case, they don't think of it as a networking opportunity. Be prepared to hand out some business cards. Don't, however, act pushy. You may appear to be pushy if you "work the room" in an attempt to promote yourself, your product, or your service.

Why Am I Here?

Before you attend, ask yourself what you hope to gain from the seminar. Here's how two new managers approached an upcoming management skills seminar.

(1) When human resources personnel notified John B. that they had made arrangements for him to attend a popular seminar program, he was suspicious. Did upper management question his ability to perform well?

(2) Alex R. asked his boss if the company would sponsor his attendance at the seminar. After four months in the new position, he had discovered that his open-door policy meant he had to work some Saturdays. He believed there must be a better way to keep communications open and still have sufficient time for uninterrupted work so he needn't come into the office on Saturdays.

John B. and Alex R. attended the same seminar.

The speaker was entertaining and informative and John B. listened. Alex R. listened carefully and waited for the speaker to discuss his specific concerns. When she did, he made notes and asked questions.

When the speaker discussed ineffective delegation skills, he recognized personal weak points. He didn't empower his staff, give them authority to act.

As a result, people didn't move from one step to the next without consulting with him. He told staff what to do but didn't say why. Since they were in the dark regarding over-all work objectives, it wasn't surprising that they approached him frequently with questions.

Both managers planned to institute changes. Alex R. used the seminar workbook and notes as reference material. He spent the next two months acting on new ideas he thought were worthwhile. Before long, he rarely worked on Saturdays and tied that achievement to what he learned at the seminar.

Eventually John B. became adept at bringing time-wasting telephone calls to a polite but prompt close. He sharpened his technique based upon the seminar trainer's demonstrations.

Each manager gained from the seminar experience and in doing so demonstrated to upper management the opportunity wasn't wasted.

When you waste or trivialize opportunities, you virtually thumb your nose at those who help to provide them by paying for your seminar and making it possible for you to attend on company time.

Alex R., however, was far more generous about demonstrating his appreciation than John B. He did everything possible to make the most of the seminar opportunity. John B. was passive, but he benefitted in spite of himself.

Enthusiasm!

Your enthusiasm translates into a subtle way to thank management for providing you with any self-enriching opportunity. Saying thanks is basic to *Everyday Business Etiquette* tenets and when you say thanks with your deeds, you leave an indelible message.

> *"Nothing great was ever achieved without enthusiasm."*
>
> Ralph Waldo Emerson

When you're enthusiastic about an upcoming seminar, you'll automatically make management feel good about sponsoring your attendance. In addition, you'll probably ask yourself what you hope to gain and be better prepared to come away with information you can use. If you sponsor your own attendance, share the news with management. Tell your boss about the experience by sharing some of what you learned. If you received a certificate of completion or a certificate which confers Continuing Education Units upon you, make a copy of it and request that it be added to your employee file.

Don't Waste Money

Did you know that seminar tuition is tax deductible? Travel dollars, meal costs, and parking expenses are also considered expenses incurred in pursuit of professional education.

If you work for a small company where it's not customary to send employees to training seminars, management may be unaware of this benefit. Show regard for the company's dollars by asking whether vouchers or other expense records should be obtained for purposes of documenting a bona fide tax deduction.

People who are careful about not wasting their own dollars sometimes show a disregard for spending company dollars. It's admirable to avoid wasting company dollars, too, and it's a trait that isn't likely to go unnoticed or unappreciated. It's another quiet way to say "thanks for underwriting me."

Evaluate the Experience

If you believe a note of thanks is in order, give your boss or the appropriate executive useful information, as well as your thanks. Rate the speaker, the content of the program, and the hotel or facility where the seminar was conducted. If you believe the experience was worthwhile and coworkers may benefit from attending, say so. If you were disappointed, be candid. No sense sending others to a seminar that isn't worthwhile. It may be that other seminar providers offer the same subject matter in a more exciting and useful format.

Some of the major seminar providers offer money back if customers aren't satisfied. If you believe the seminar was a waste of time, you may want to suggest the company request a refund.

Plan to take notes that enable you to make a useful evaluation. You'll be able to refer to them if you put an evaluation into writing or if your boss asks you, "How was it?"

When you say, "The speaker was great but the hotel was a disaster. There weren't sufficient parking spaces and I drove around for fifteen minutes before I found a space at the outer edge of the parking lot. It took me another few minutes to walk to the meeting room. Dining-room service was so slow at lunch time that I didn't have time to finish my sandwich," you paint a vivid picture.

Management may think twice before sending someone off to a seminar at that hotel again, or may decide if the speaker was great then it's a good idea to arrange for the speaker to do an on-site seminar. In short, your detailed observations perform a service. They certainly don't compare with an "It was okay" answer, which essentially says nothing.

ON-THE-CAREER-PATH TIPS

- Read Chapter Seven: Send a Message with Your Wardrobe Selections
- Read Chapter Twelve: Correspondence

STRATEGY YOU CAN USE

Obtain and read the marketing material the seminar provider generates. It highlights benefits and probably outlines the program. You'll have time to think about how this seminar can help you before you attend. Experts claim you gain much more from seminar attendance when you funnel general information down to address your specific needs. If you've read the materials beforehand, you'll be ready to do so.

Sometimes you're told what to expect when you arrive at the seminar location. If, for example, you must pay for parking, you'll be notified and can have cash handy. If the seminar price doesn't include lunch, you may not want to buy lunch at a pricey hotel restaurant and you can brown-bag it or make other arrangements. Most seminars are copyrighted and you'll probably be told not to record the program.

You don't want to be caught short of cash or embarrassed by being asked to leave your recording equipment at the back of the room. All your preparation efforts enable you to keep your gentility in fine working condition!

WHEN YOU'RE AWAY FROM THE OFFICE WITH YOUR BOSS

You're accompanying your boss so you can assist him or her in much the same way you do in the office. The difference is you're working together in atypical surroundings. You may dine together, travel in a taxi together, or join customers or clients at a bar or restaurant. As a result, you'll have to call upon some expanded business etiquette know-how.

- Can you quit at 5:00 P.M. or are you expected to have dinner with the boss?
- If you're going to be in a city that has a special attraction (e.g., jazz in New Orleans, Broadway shows in New York) and know you'll have time to take advantage of it, should you go alone or does courtesy demand that you invite the boss?
- Should you offer to pay for lunch or pay your share?

- If the boss says a prayer of thanks before eating a meal, must you bow your head, too?
- If the boss doesn't introduce you to a customer, should you extend your hand and introduce yourself?

How would you decide to handle these situations?

Make decisions based upon your relationship with your boss. If you're both women, it's less complicated to decide that you'll dine together and see a show than if one of you is a man. An evening spent participating in nonbusiness pursuits may offer the wrong impression to others (including your boss). On the other hand, if you're accustomed to socializing with the boss from time to time on your home turf, there's probably no reason to shy away from doing so when you're away from the office.

Make decisions based upon your priorities. If you worked hard all day and would prefer to order a room-service meal and telephone your spouse and youngsters at home, don't feel obligated to do otherwise. On the other hand, job success is a priority, too, and if your boss expects you to join him or her for drinks or dinner, you may not want to risk offending the boss by refusing the invitation.

Some questions have simple answers.

It's not necessary for you to bow your head or pray with someone else. It's courteous to wait silently for someone to finish praying. Once you know this individual says grace before meals, you show respect by waiting for him or her to do so before starting to eat your food.

When it comes to personal expenses, don't assume the boss is covering your costs. Offer to pay your share if the company doesn't always reimburse for all expenses and you don't know whether meals are covered. One young executive insists that people equate money with power and buys her boss lunch from time to time just to remind him that he's not the only one with power. You may or may not find merit in her philosophy but from an *Everyday Business Etiquette* position, it's polite not to take anyone or anything for granted. Say thank you when the boss pays for your mealtime expenses even when you believe the company will reimburse the boss. If you purchase candy bars, chewing gum, newspapers, or other small items for yourself, buy some for the boss, too. You'll demonstrate that generosity is not a one-way street.

It's both permissible and appropriate to introduce yourself to a customer if the boss fails to introduce you. Assume it was an oversight and extend your hand to the individual for a handshake and announce your name.

Oh, Oh, Oh

When you're away from the office with your boss you may discover small idiosyncrasies you'd probably never discover at the office.

- He may, for example, stir the sugar into his coffee until you think the china cup will be worn thin and spring a leak.
- She may, for example, hum loudly while she eats dessert.
- He may doze off during a van ride to the airport and suck on his finger.
- She may take off her shoes whenever she rides on an escalator.

You're in a position of trust and should restrain yourself from revealing these oddities to others. Even though it's tempting to let someone else know the boss is vulnerable (and you're not exactly giving away company secrets), it's poor form to compromise anyone by revealing his or her idiosyncrasies to others.

Surname or Not Surname, That Is the Question

You may work in a very informal office where everyone, boss included, is called by his or her first name. When you travel away from the office, it may be appropriate to call your boss by his or her surname and refer to the boss by surname when you speak with others, too.

"*Si fueris Romae, Romano vivito more; Si fueris alibi, vivito sicut ibi.*" When you are at Rome live in the Roman style; when you are elsewhere live as they live elsewhere.

Your boss should appreciate your quick assessment of the new environment in which you're working and may take your lead and refer to you by your surname.

If you normally use surnames when addressing one another and arrive at an office where people are more informal, don't switch gears and call your boss by his or her first name. Although you're unlikely to offend your boss by moving from a less formal to a more formal manner of address, you risk offending the boss if you move in the other direction.

As much as we like to apply good advice across the board, it can't always be done. This leads to another bit of advice: Have faith in your own good judgment!

Safe Topics of Conversation

Use your good judgment when it comes to small talk, too. No matter whether you're engaging in light, pass-the-time conversation with your boss or with people with whom your boss is conducting business, stay away from topics that may be inflammatory. Money, religion, and politics are some topics you'll want to avoid. The natural beauty of the location to which you have traveled, your opinion regarding a popular movie, or comments about favorite musicians or artists, sports, weather conditions, the last good book you read, are likely to be safer topics on which to expound.

You certainly don't want to act paranoid, but it would be naive to disregard the possibility that someone may try to pump you for information which could give him or her the upper hand during delicate negotiations with your boss. An individual's attempts to do so may even be overt and you may feel offended.

Since you're acting as a support person, you're in a sensitive position and aren't at liberty to respond to this individual in the same way you might if you were acting alone.

If possible, smile politely and extricate yourself from this individual's presence without letting him or her know how you assess such behavior. You may or may not want to tell your boss what has transpired since the boss has to stay focused on goals and you may not want to add to the burden.

If you're actually confronted with this challenge, it's comforting to know your comportment and command of business etiquette enables you to disarm the other person, defuse the situation, and maintain a level playing field so that your boss can move ahead to achieve goals. Take a bow!

Who Are You?

During work hours, you're not who you think you are!

You represent your boss and your company and your actions reflect on them.

You may find yourself taking a coffee break with individuals whose boss is conducting business with your boss.

If each person washes his or her coffee cup, wash your cup. If people contribute coins towards the purchase of coffee and condiments, make a contribution. If you overpower the conversation or appear to be a know-it-all, you're not likely to make a favorable impression and that can't benefit your boss, or his or her mission. Don't forget to say thank you.

You may have to use someone's fax machine, desk space, telephone, or supplies to complete assignments. If you move someone's papers or materials, return things to their original positions. Don't rummage through drawers or closets to find supplies. Ask for assistance and, when appropriate, ask for permission. Show respect for other people's property and don't forget to offer your thanks.

You may be asked your opinion about what these people consider their state-of-the-art manufacturing facility or their new city convention center. Pause. Ask yourself if your opinion is favorable. If so, go ahead and answer. If not, look for something pleasant to say. Tell people the good news and if there's bad news, you may want to dilute it before serving. Remember, you're acting as an agent for others and it may not be prudent to be completely frank. If you can't think of how to answer a question, don't. Turn the tables on the interrogator and ask for his or her opinion. Listen carefully. Not only may you learn something useful, to do otherwise would demonstrate insincerity and that's something you want to avoid.

 ON-THE-CAREER-PATH TIPS

- Read Chapter One: Traveling to Distant Places to Conduct Business
- Read Chapter Three: Dining-Table Etiquette You Didn't Learn at Home
- Read Chapter Five: Courteous Behavior with Members of the Opposite Sex
- Read Chapter Seven: Send a Message with Your Wardrobe Selections

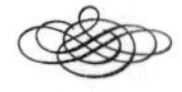 STRATEGY YOU CAN USE

Consider an invitation from the boss to you to accompany him or her on a business mission away from the office as a vote of confidence in you and your ability to perform. Let that observation serve to buoy your spirits. By accentuating the positive, you'll find it easier to allay concerns you may have about working in a new and different environment. Instead, you'll focus on using this opportunity to show the boss that this confidence isn't misplaced.

HOSTING BUSINESSPEOPLE FROM OTHER COUNTRIES

Tackle this assignment the same way you tackle any assignment.

1. *Identify preferences and priorities. What do the visitors hope to achieve? What does company management want to achieve? Is it realistic to believe you can satisfy all parties? If not, work with management to adjust goals until they're realistic. Then you're ready to proceed.*

2. *Acquaint yourself with time considerations. Reach beyond the usual question: How many days will the visitors be with us?—and find out about the size of the group and its preparedness.*

   If, for example, your visitor is a single individual, you'll move about together with greater ease than if the group constitutes a party of twelve. Moreover, if individuals speak English or you're fluent in the visitor's language, you won't need to allow extra time for interpretations.

   Have members of the group visited your part of the world before? Find out. Familiarity or lack of it will impact time parameters, too.

   It helps to know if the visitors are participant types or spectator types. Participant types may not enjoy spending hours traveling from place to place in a bus whereas spectator types may delight in the tour experience.

3. *Execute a plan to achieve goals. If this is a goodwill, getting-to-know-you-better visit, you'll design a different plan than if it's a signing-the-contract kind of visit.*

4. *Review, evaluate. Remember, there's a middle to this assignment, as well as a beginning and an end. During the visit, take time to evaluate your plan and alter it, if necessary. If visitors send negative signals (e.g., they're tired or unenthusiastic), you may want to solicit their recommendations and make adjustments.*

5. *Don't be afraid to make changes but do take care not to toss goal attainment out the window.*

Get Down to Business

All of the above represent courteous actions. That's because they insure you're not going to waste anyone's time. When people make a long trip to conduct business, it's especially considerate to be efficient so the effort is worthwhile for all concerned. Of course, this doesn't mean selling people your widgets at a below-cost price, but it does mean doing everything within your power to be a gracious host or hostess. When you represent your company, your actions reflect upon everyone in the company and impact how they're viewed by others.

Don't underestimate the importance of this assignment. Prepare as best you can and then, if things go wrong, be ready to meet challenges with a light heart and a concern for the well-being of your visitors. Even when people don't share the same language they often share the ability to laugh at awkward situations. Laughter can be the pause that refreshes.

Action, Please!

Most foreign visitors have preconceived notions about life in the United States of America. Once visitors arrive, they'll see and hear many things first hand. Here are some activities you may want to incorporate into their schedule so they can get into the action rather than base their information solely upon reading, hearing, and viewing on the big screen.

Home, please! If at all possible, plan to invite the foreign business people to your home or to the home of one of the company executives. If the group is small and includes a spouse and children, invite them, too. If the group is large and no one's home will accommodate the group at the same time, you may want to divide and conquer. Plan two or three different home excursions by enlisting the services of two or three company executives and prevailing upon them to open up their homes.

Be considerate and think about what you would appreciate if conditions were reversed. You'd probably have your fill of hotel food and catered affairs and long for the simplicity of a simple home-cooked meal. How about a stroll in your vegetable garden or an opportunity to listen to your favorite music, a chance to pet a dog, or a cat, to rock in a chair on the front porch?

It may be that your foreign visitors would happily embrace the simple pleasures of home life. If guests have been traveling away from their home for some time, this is perhaps the warmest and most thoughtful invitation you can extend.

If the visitor is somewhat relaxed about formalities, you might invite him or her to fix soup and a sandwich along with you and your spouse, and even to help set the table.

Consider inviting a neighbor or close friend to join you and your visitor. The third party motivates you to give business conversation a rest, at least for the duration of the get-together.

Watch out for different tastes. Commercially prepared white bread, for example, is widely reported to be a source of surprise to many foreign visitors. Some people find it and certain other American foods distasteful.

Your foreign business visitor may be unfamiliar with sugar that's served in packets, tea inside bags, and salad dressing in squeeze bottles.

He or she may prefer food to be more highly seasoned or less highly seasoned and prefer to eat a large meal midday and a light supper at the end of the day. Your foreign guest may expect to eat lunch later than noontime and may be guided by a different clock when it comes to time to rise in the morning or retire at night. Some of these differences may also surface when you entertain guests from some distant corner of the United States. Many of the differences, however, relate directly to the habits the person shares with most of his or her own countrymen and women.

You can take steps to learn about your visitor's culture in advance, but you probably won't be able to anticipate all eventualities. Be a good listener and a good student. Your guest may be able to tell you what's missing or what has been misunderstood. If not, however, it may be due to the fact that your guest is exercising his or her own good manners and does not want to offend you.

Be aware that a guest may thank you fervently for inviting him or her to your home and never follow up with a thank-you note. In some countries (e.g., Mexico), mailed thank-you notes aren't customary.

See the sights, please! Another way to entertain your foreign business guests is by introducing them to the sights and sounds of your hometown or the company's locale. When you arrange a visit to a local park, main library, college campus, city hall, shopping mall, or firehouse, you demonstrate pride in your community.

Scan the entertainment pages of your local newspaper to locate events—a college ballgame, dedication festivities for a new ice-skating rink, a concert performance at a local church, a special meeting of the local garden club. The more commonplace the activity, the more meaningful it is likely to be to your foreign business visitors.

When appropriate, alert event organizers or sponsors in advance that you'll arrive with special guests. It may earn you and your guests some red-carpet treatment and a behind the scenes look at a facility.

Your creativity in selecting off-beat sights and sounds for your visitor's edification should be appreciated. When your guests feel happy and enthusiastic about their stay, it's natural that those good feelings spill over to business discussions and decision-making. So your short-lived career as host enables you to advance business goals.

Be practical, please! Don't feel compelled to keep your guest entertained every waking minute. The business visitor may feel it would be poor form to say no thanks when you suggest an activity. As a result, he or she may actually be worn out and you may be tired, too, but neither party confesses! You'll have to step lightly around this possible dilemma. Otherwise, you may appear to be inattentive.

Crime is not a pleasant subject but it's courteous and considerate, as well as practical, to alert your foreign business guest to be aware of places in the city which aren't considered safe. You may want to point out that it's unwise to enter dark alleyways that appear to be deserted or display large amounts of cash in the hotel lobby or other public places. You don't want the visitor to think you underestimate his or her good judgment, so take care. A general crime alert is probably sufficient unless you're asked to provide details or unless you believe the individual is so unsophisticated that he or she is an accident waiting to happen. If that's the case, you'll probably want to confer with your boss or a colleague to determine how best to proceed. When it comes to *Everyday Business Etiquette* assessment, you have some responsibility to the guest for his or her well-being, especially because you're better informed than the traveler about the personal safety requirements of your area.

Foreign business people may want to attend religious services, especially if they're away from their own places of worship for any length of time. If someone questions you about religion in your country, don't automatically avoid the subject. Even though it's popularly suggested that one avoid discussing religion or politics in the business environment, it may be the individual is bringing up the subject to find out how to make arrangements to attend a religious service.

(Do you know the story about the child who asked his Dad, "Where do I come from?" The father struggled to explain the birth process when the child only wanted to know the name of the city of his birth.)

If you do assist the traveler to locate worship services to attend, take care that you understand exactly what's required since it's usually not sufficient to know, for example, that an individual is Jewish, Baptist or Roman Catholic. Present the local telephone classified pages to your visitor, so that he or she is made aware of what's available in the area. If necessary, make telephone calls to clergy in order to obtain answers to your visitor's questions, but don't feel that you must accompany the individual to services. You aren't bending any rules of etiquette if you don't join your guest unless he or she specifically asks you to do so. If you don't care to accept the invitation, feel free to decline, but be available to escort the guest to and from the services. It's possible you were invited along so the guest could rely upon you to deal with logistics. If that's true, your offer to act as an escort will solve the problem. It's an opportunity for you to demonstrate you're willing to go the extra step, and helps you to strengthen the relationship and build trust, both of which bode well for future business dealings.

Too Much of a Good Thing

"Can we ever have too much of a good thing?" You don't want to smother your guests from other lands with so much attention that they answer this question in the affirmative!

On the other hand, in a social setting it's easy to forget that business associates are not personal friends. When you invite someone to your home or escort him or her to entertainment events, the distinction can blur.

- Maintain reasonable dress and grooming habits at all times while with the visitor. (Don't appear at your breakfast table at home without a shave or dressed in a frayed pair of jeans.)
- If you're a smoker, take care to exercise courteous smoking habits that are not normally applied when you're with friends and family. (Don't reserve a table in the smoking section of the restaurant if your guest isn't a smoker.)
- If your guest is status-conscious, he or she may feel uncomfortable riding in your family car if it's an economy model or shows signs of family members' use such as toys or dog hairs in the back seat or finger marks on the windows. Surprised? Don't be. Some folks live in an environment where material accoutrements help define their position. The cost of a snazzy rental car for the duration of the guest's stay is probably far less than the cost of offending the individual, albeit, quite unintentionally. Perhaps, an appropriate company car can be made available to you.

ON-THE-CAREER-PATH TIPS

- Read Chapter Fourteen: Other Languages, Other Niceties, Other Resources

STRATEGY YOU CAN USE

If you don't feel entirely comfortable about accepting this assignment, see if you can cohost with someone who may be more experienced and therefore more confident. If that's not possible, try contacting an individual who can act as advisor. Don't hesitate to confer with the company human resource director to locate a recently retired individual who may have a wealth of experience and the time to act as your mentor. You don't want to tackle this assignment with a practice-makes-perfect attitude. It's not the best time for a practice run since there's so much opportunity for misunderstandings.

If you work with a "mentor," he or she deserves a small gift along with your thanks when the foreign business people depart. Do tell this person something about your experience as a host, as he or she probably will want to know but may be too polite to inquire.

WHEN HIGH-LEVEL BUSINESS DEALS CALL FOR HIGH-SOCIETY KNOW-HOW

"I suppose society is wonderfully delightful. To be in it is merely a bore. But to be out of it simply a tragedy."

Oscar Wilde, *A Woman of No Importance,* 1893

In the world of business, it's nothing short of a tragedy to be left out!

That's the risk you run when you travel on a corporate jet, spend a weekend at your boss's country estate, board a yacht to attend a dinner party hosted by a major client, or participate in any other rarified-setting occasion if you disregard the accepted code of conduct.

According to Ms. Dorothea Johnson, Director of The Protocol School of Washington® in McLean, Virginia, who is an authority on corporate etiquette and international protocol, "It's embarrassing when the flight attendant has to tell a young executive to please vacate seats in a private airplane since they're reserved for the CEO and his guest of honor."

Yet several private airplane flight attendants who have attended Ms. Johnson's classes attest to the fact that many younger executives sit in the first seats they find. Furthermore, when the flight attendant asks them to move, they resist.

It's not surprising that Johnson cautions her clients to ask the flight attendant, "Where shall I sit?" She also advises, "Don't ask for anything that isn't offered."

"The flight attendant may say, 'Can I get you a soda or a glass of wine?' That's a clear indication that there's not any hard alcohol on board."

Nevertheless, flight attendants report that some young executives reply, "I'll have a scotch and water."

"Often wine isn't offered. If you're asked, 'May I get you something to drink, mineral water or soda?', that's a clear indication there's no alcohol on the plane.

"And often the plane will have absolutely no smoking, but some executives seem to ignore this protocol."

According to Ms. Johnson, you put someone on the spot if you ask, 'May I smoke?' Remember this, too, when you're on terra firma and in someone's office. "If there are no ashtrays, that is a silent signal there's no smoking. If there are ashtrays in a board room, for example, and the Chief Executive Officer is smoking, that's a clear signal that others may smoke. If not, don't ask!"

Ms. Johnson stresses the importance of not putting someone on the spot with a question he or she may prefer to answer in the negative when you obviously expect a green-light-go-ahead.

Finally, don't leave anything behind when you exit the plane. This includes paper, litter, jackets, ties, and shoes!

One attendant reports that someone actually left a pair of shoes on the floor in front of his seat. It's assumed he didn't exit in bare feet.

You won't feel relaxed and able to perform well if you feel stifled by too many "do nots" but these "do nots" enable you to remain composed and demonstrate finesse even though travel in a private plane is not your everyday activity.

To Sum Up

When you're invited to travel on a private plane:

- Ask the flight attendant or your host where you should sit.
- Don't ask for anything that isn't offered. Your good manners shine when you're observant and listen carefully to the flight attendant. If he or she is vague, and asks an open-ended question such as "May I get something for you to drink?", ask "What would you suggest?"

  Ms. Johnson advises executives of all ages to think with their eyes, ears, and minds.
- Don't smoke. The only time you may consider smoking is when your host or hostess smokes or invites you to do so.
- Don't litter or leave personal possessions behind. You demonstrate your respect for another person's property when you treat it with care.

When the Address Is No Ordinary Address

You may be invited to someone's country home, private estate, or villa for the very first time and wonder how you'll know what's expected.

According to corporate etiquette specialist Dorothea Johnson, the savvy host or hostess will tell you what's planned in advance.

"If you're invited for the weekend, you may be told, 'Please arrive by five o'clock on Friday because we're having a cocktail party at six and dinner at seven o'clock'."

She tells her clients they should also supply some type of agenda to guests upon arrival to reinforce the earlier message.

Don't be surprised to receive a schedule of planned activities when you arrive.

"I've seen [this method used] in a lot of private homes, large estates where I have visited and not only in this country but in other countries.

"If you're invited for a weekend in the country and not given any indication as to what is going to happen, it's proper to pick up the telephone and call the host or hostess and say thank you for inviting me and I would like to know what clothes I should bring . . ."

In addition to knowing something about what's planned for the duration of your stay, try to learn as much as possible about the person or persons who are entertaining you.

"What I tell everyone is whether it's for entertainment or for meeting someone for a discussion which may lead to a future business relationship, always find out as much as possible about the person you'll be dealing with."

It's not only appropriate to telephone a personal secretary or administrative assistant and ask for assistance, it's smart!

Call. Introduce yourself. Explain that you're going to be a guest at Mr. or Ms. Chief Executive's country home or estate at such-and-such time and explain that you'd like to bring an appropriate gift. Inquire about the number of children in the family. Ask if there are any likes or dislikes you should know about. You might want to learn whether or not your hosts play golf or tennis.

Most corporations have an organizational chart that indicates the levels of command. Obtain a copy from the human resources director and you'll be better prepared for your meeting with a company executive to discuss business.

When you contact an individual's assistant to learn more about him or her or contact other company personnel, a poised and confident manner should guarantee cooperation. Provide as many details about yourself and the circumstances as possible so the person you're speaking with knows it's a bona fide inquiry.

Gift Time

Always bring a gift for your host unless you know very little about that person's taste, or never met his or her spouse and know little or nothing about that person's preferences, either. Since you'll know more after you've spent time together, it's permissible to choose a gift later, but do so with dispatch and arrange for a prompt delivery.

Ms. Johnson tries to "fit the gift to the personality of the family."

"If it's a family with children, I try to make it a gift the entire family would enjoy. If I want to separate the children's gifts from the parents, I would give the parents a joint gift and then give the children individual gifts."

When it comes to determining what would make an appropriate gift, you'll have to rely upon your own creativity. It's not necessary and may not be appropriate to spend a good deal of money for the gift and it may be more of a challenge to decide on a gift for people who seem to have everything. As a result you have a special opportunity to demonstrate your style.

Let your imagination roam freely and you may find yourself shopping in the local book and music shop or gravitating to places you favor when shopping for yourself. If your friends delight in sharing the bounty from your fruit trees, for example, take or send a small gift to the host family along with an elegantly printed I-Owe-You note for a bushel of grapefruit or apples when the trees yield fruit. Of course, you'll have to remember to deliver on your promise.

What Is There To See?

It's possible that you'll find yourself in a beautiful natural setting and want to explore. You may have heard that your hosts have a stable and own fine horses. If you'd like to wander the grounds, Ms. Johnson advises not to do so without asking permission first.

"I would say something such as, 'I would love to take a walk. Is it all right if I walk near the barn?'"

Experience suggests one is generally guided around the estate and not left to wander off alone. Don't leap to the conclusion that because you're a guest, you're free to meander. It's presumptuous and demonstrates poor form.

To Sum Up

- Don't suffer in silence if you haven't a clue as to what to pack or what to expect when you arrive for the weekend. You're not breaking the rules of etiquette if you make an inquiry.

- Always give a gift. Try to avoid generic-type gifts. Use the occasion to supply something the entire host family can enjoy.

- Learn as much as possible about people before you spend time with them. The more you know, the more you'll be able to address the individual's specific interests and needs. It's a vital component of business success and *Everyday Business Etiquette* enthusiastically echoes the Scout's motto: Be prepared!

You're Invited to Attend a Yacht Party!

According to Ms. Johnson, "The rule to remember is: the person who owns or leases the yacht is the captain."

The captain is in charge! Follow instructions. Before the yacht party you'll probably receive a note asking you to wear rubber-soled shoes. Don't assume your host is a difficult person acting in a capricious or arbitrary fashion. If you wear leather-soled shoes you can easily slip on the deck since decks are typically polished to a high gloss. Moreover, leather-soled shoes can damage the deck.

What should you wear in addition to rubber-soled shoes?

Check your invitation for further directions regarding attire. If you don't receive any, it's permissible to ask what's expected. If you're told the party is informal, it usually means sports clothes for both genders. Be aware of the different levels of sports clothes. When you host an affair on a yacht, do remember to tell your guests something about appropriate personal attire so they can feel comfortable about their personal appearance when they arrive.

If the captain (your host) announces a particular time for lunch or dinner, show up at the appointed time. This may mean disengaging yourself from some activity at the far end of a large yacht to get to the dining room or galley in a timely fashion. Do it!

Guests who disregard this request are inconsiderate. A host who is coordinating the affair isn't likely to take kindly to this do-your-own-thing response since he or she is charged with the care and feeding of everyone in attendance and lack of cooperation makes the job more difficult.

To Sum Up

- Cooperate with your host by paying careful attention to requests. On a yacht, expect to wear rubber-soled shoes.
- Remember casual attire often translates to "black-tie" dress rather than shorts and a pullover shirt.
- Arrive at the dining table on time so as not to inconvenience anyone.

Brush Up on Your Dining Skills

No matter where high level business gatherings take place, food and drink are likely to be served. In any gracious setting, food and beverage presentation is likely to be lavish.

- Don't help yourself to the bounty without being specifically invited to do so.
- When there's buffet service, don't fill your plate too full and take care not to lean across the table and violate the space occupied by other guests.
- When in doubt as to which utensil to use or how to perform some other table technique, casually observe how several others conduct themselves. Don't rely strictly on one person's approach as he or she may not be correct. Be a careful observer and you'll soon have the information you need to proceed with ease.

ON-THE-CAREER-PATH TIPS

- Read Chapter One: Hosting Business People from Other Countries, and Preparing for Black-tie Business Functions
- Read Chapter Three: Dining-Table Etiquette You Didn't Learn at Home
- Read Chapter Four: Mastering Nonverbal Communication
- Read Chapter Eight: Invitations; Chapter Nine: Gifts; and Chapter Ten: Introductions

STRATEGY YOU CAN USE

> *"The superior man is satisfied and composed; the mean man is always full of distress."*
>
> Confucius (551–479 B.C.)

You may be unaccustomed to being a guest in an ambience associated with great wealth. Relax. You're invited! Plan to enjoy yourself. Rely on your smile, good posture, pleasant tone of voice, and firm handshake to convey your outward composure to others. A composed-you equals a superior-you—someone who is ready, willing and able to perform well in any environment. Rely upon your preparation and powers of observation to help you navigate the course.

If you often conduct business in glamorous surroundings, take care to make young executives and others you invite comfortable by tactfully informing them about what to expect (i.e., agenda, proper attire). While you may be watching to see how younger executives perform, you may be slightly out of step with your performance as a host if you don't work to make the occasion as pleasant as possible for everyone in attendance.

WORKING VIA AN INTERPRETER

If you speak only one language well, you may be in awe of those who have great facility with two or more languages. Their accomplishment may appear to be so enormous that you're tempted to dispense with mundane questions when you prepare to hire an individual to bridge communications between you and foreign business contacts.

Stop.

You owe it to yourself and to those with whom you conduct business to engage a professional interpreter who maintains high standards.

You'll want to make certain that:

- The interpreter is comfortable and up to date with the pertinent languages and conversant with industry-specific terms. If you're talking about steam-turbine generators, for example, the interpreter should not be a stranger to this subject matter.
- If proprietary or confidential information is discussed, the interpreter will maintain confidentiality. You may want it understood that no matter what is discussed, the interpreter will treat all communication as confidential.

Associates should feel confident that you have taken reasonable steps to engage someone eminently qualified to perform well.

If the interpreter will be at your side almost constantly, it's important that he or she be dressed and groomed appropriately to blend in to the setting. Your invitation to the opera or a formal dinner is extended to the interpreter, too. It's unrealistic to expect the interpreter to behave as though he or she were an inanimate object, especially when attending a social function. On the other hand, it's reasonable to expect the interpreter to refrain from engaging in long, private conversations with your business contacts.

If you live or work in a large city, you may find the expert you need listed in the Yellow Pages of your telephone directory.

The American Translators Association (ATA) in Alexandria, Virginia, founded in 1959, is reported to be the largest professional association of translators and interpreters in the United States, with over 5,500 members. The ATA *Translation Services Directory* (TSD) is published annually and "contains professional profiles of active and corresponding members who accept translating or interpreting assignments; indexes by language, subject, and geographic location."

The TSD contains 148 areas of specialization, from arts to zoology, and 110 language combinations, from Albanian to Vietnamese. So you shouldn't have to settle for anything less than a perfect match!

It's important to note that a translator and an interpreter are not necessarily one and the same. Translators typically work with written words and if you have business material that must be committed to paper in a language in which you're not fluent, you'll probably engage a translator.

The American Translators Association [1800 Diagonal Road, Suite 220, Alexandria, VA 22314, (703) 683-6100] also publishes a 12-page booklet, "A Consumer's Guide to Good Translation," (Price: $5.00) that you may find helpful.

Cooperation Is More Than a Courteous Plan

An experienced interpreter will assist you to prepare for an assignment. If you think of him or her as a member of your team you'll both be better prepared to accomplish goals.

The interpreter will want to know answers to many questions:

- Where will discussions take place? On a stage in front of an audience? Around a conference table?
- Will microphones be necessary? If so, will the interpreter be supplied with one so that it's unnecessary to pass a microphone back and forth?
- If microphones aren't used, will each participant be able to hear well, including the interpreter? If, for example, you participate in a panel discussion which takes place in a warehouse environment, might sounds get lost in the cavernous setting? It's essential that the interpreter be able to hear all the speakers well.
- Where will the interpreter be located? Seated or standing? Will a table with ample lighting and drinking water be available for the interpreter's use? (Some interpreters take notes.)

How Can You Help?

- It's important for you to convey a complete idea as opposed to frequently pausing or stopping mid-sentence. You may want to use a tape recorder to capture five or ten minutes of a presentation. Listen to your delivery and if you're inclined to pause often, alert the interpreter to this tendency in your speaking style.
- Do pause between paragraphs. If it's not something you typically do, plan to do so when working with an interpreter.
- Don't look at the interpreter when you speak. Keep your eyes on the audience. If you don't, your message loses impact on your listeners.
- When it's your turn to listen, look at the person who is speaking to you even though you don't understand the words. When the interpreter translates, you may want to transfer your gaze to the interpreter but it's permissible to rivet your attention on your foreign language speaking business contact. Body language talks, too, and you don't want to miss anything.
- It's difficult to translate jokes without running the risk of making a mistake and causing offense. If you're convinced that a joke or topical comment is necessary, you may want to check with your interpreter in advance and give him or her time to research the presentation so that it doesn't boomerang. Language translation faux pas have ranged from comical to offensive to embarrassing to ridiculous and have been reported in sufficient numbers to fill books.
- Ask your interpreter if it would help to agree upon one or two signals to permit you to privately communicate with one another about how the translation is progressing. An up-and-down head motion, for example, may alert you to slow down.
- Be yourself. Your body language communicates with the interpreter as well as with the audience and you shouldn't be tempted to alter your presentation simply because you're talking to people who can't understand your spoken language.
- Ask the interpreter if there's anything he or she would like to suggest and listen carefully to the response. If you can't agree to some requests, say so. Candid communication between yourself and this individual is necessary.

- You may want to thank the interpreter publicly. A brief thanks is all that is necessary at the end of the day's activities if more is planned for the next day. A more generous thank-you can be reserved for the conclusion of the gathering.
- When you discuss the interpreter's schedule and fee, you may want to include time for a brief evaluation session prior to the conclusion of the assignment.

Although the interpreter acts only to support free-flowing communication between people who don't share the same spoken language, he or she may be able to offer advice on how to improve communications in the future. Since body language and other nuances combine with the spoken word to send messages, the interpreter's observations may help you to assess all that has transpired.

An Interpreter's Assistance

Sam T. hired an interpreter when he had to conduct business in Paris. He felt that something was amiss when a two-hour dinnertime meeting with a potential client ended. He asked the interpreter for an assessment and discovered the interpreter thought the meeting ended abruptly. She suggested that Sam T. avoid giving signs that he was ready to leave (i.e., removing his napkin from his lap, repeatedly checking his wristwatch, and fidgeting with his empty coffee cup). She indicated to Sam that dinnertime get-togethers in Paris generally last a long time.

When Sam T. went to the individual's office the next morning, he explained that he believed he was taking too much of the man's valuable time when they dined, especially since he knew they'd meet again early in the morning. He then moved on to praise the food served in Paris and soon got back on track with business topics.

At the end of the morning meeting, Sam T. had a new client!

Robert L. was in Monterrey, Mexico, visiting a business contact he'd met once before in Chicago. The man was more comfortable speaking Spanish and although Robert had some command of the Spanish language, he engaged an interpreter to be present when they discussed business. They conversed at length during a lunch meeting, but later that day, Robert L. was notified that future meetings were cancelled. He was baffled and telephoned the interpreter who inquired as to whether or not Robert L. knew that one's wardrobe is very important in Mexico since it's equated with showing respect for the other person. She indicated that Robert's pink tie and missing jacket may have been perceived as offensive. She hesitated, but finally added that Robert's undershirt was visible beneath his unbuttoned shirt collar when he loosened his tie toward the end of the meal. Robert recalled the temperature climbed while they dined on the patio and he was surprised that others didn't remove their jackets.

Robert L. never discovered whether or not the interpreter was correct but it took him two years to win the Mexican contact's favor. He was especially attentive to his wardrobe selections and shed his casual behavior when they spent time together in Chicago or in Monterrey.

Sam T. and Robert L. are fictional characters but there's nothing fictional about the pitfalls described.

You may benefit from the words of wisdom an interpreter can offer but it's far better to be prepared well in advance of your meeting. Remember, too, that face-to-face communications can be misunderstood owing to cultural differences. If, for example, your contact's decisions are typically more dependent upon group consensus, he or she may be indirect and noncommittal when communicating with you. Nevertheless, someone's overtones, subtleties, and intimations can hint at his or her evaluation of your terms and often send a message to those fluent in the language. Whether or not you get the message may depend largely upon your interpreter's skills.

You may want to learn enough of the foreign language to ask your contact whether or not he or she is pleased with the interpreter's performance. Step lightly. Your inquiry may be perceived as too bold. Moreover, it would be unseemly to inquire within earshot of the interpreter. So, while your interests are best served when you work with an excellent interpreter, don't compromise business etiquette to obtain a second opinion.

ON-THE-CAREER-PATH TIPS

- Read Chapter One: Hosting Businesspeople from Other Countries
- Read Chapter Four: Mastering Nonverbal Communication
- Read Chapter Six: At-the-Podium Protocol
- Read Chapter Seven: Send a Message with Your Wardrobe Selections. (Take note that business-dress codes or expectations vary somewhat from country to country.)
- Read Chapter Fourteen: Other Languages, Other Niceties, Other Resources

STRATEGY YOU CAN USE

Conducting business in another country and in another language is a challenge. Maintain a sensible personal-care regimen and you should be more than equal to the task. If you normally jog, swim, ride an exercise bicycle, or play tennis, don't assume you can't or shouldn't participate in the activity just because you're away from home. Exercise! If necessary, order bottled water, avoid foods you judge to be too exotic for your constitution, and get sufficient rest. It's a strategy that works at home or away but it's especially worthy of note whenever you're juggling special challenges and may be tempted to ignore personal-care needs. Don't!

PREPARING FOR BLACK-TIE BUSINESS FUNCTIONS

The rules of etiquette are somewhat inflexible when it comes to dressing for a black-tie business function and your options are narrow. Although you may seek assistance from a formal-wear sales or rental representative who should be well informed regarding current fashion dictates, it's wise to have some grasp of the possibilities before you assemble your ensemble!

Bow tie. Pleated white shirt. Vest or waistcoat. Braces (i.e., suspenders). Cummerbund. Tuxedo. Shiny, plain-toe shoes. Cuff links and studs. Pocket square. These are special-occasion components of a businessman's attire. If this outfit is already part of your wardrobe, you'll want to examine it for readiness (i.e., style, fit, and condition).

At one time formal attire referred to white tie as opposed to black tie. If you attend a benefit dinner, official public affair, debutante party, or a ball, a tailcoat and white tie may be required. If the words "black tie" appear on the invitation, it means you're expected to wear a tuxedo. A black-tie occasion usually calls for semiformal clothing albeit, some people consider a tuxedo sufficiently formal.

Businesswomen preparing to attend a black-tie business function will obviously make different wardrobe choices but will dress in semiformal fashion. A revealing gown or cocktail dress shouldn't be worn to a business function.

When you thumb through your local telephone book to locate formal-wear establishments, you may notice a reference to "Consumer Tips." If you're a USWest customer, for example, you will find the following "EasySource Consumer Tips": "The Right Tux," "Proper Attire" and "It's A Wedding." You may pick up useful information if you follow dialing instructions and listen to the recorded message. Brite Voice Systems, Inc. provides the tips for USWest customers (US West Marketing Resources Group, Inc., Englewood, Colorado).

If you feel you must make an in-depth study of formal wear you may want to obtain a copy of *The Elegant Man* (*How to Construct the Ideal Wardrobe*) by Riccardo Villarosa and Giuliano Angeli (NY: Random House, 1990). This book contains information on fabric cut and tailoring, maintenance and care, and devotes approximately twenty pages to the subject of "Specific Occasions."

Style and grace are the underpinning of business etiquette and when you're called upon to participate at a formal function, you should make every effort to display your own style and grace. The correct attire assists you to rise to the occasion.

Formal Attire, From the Bottom, Up

When you're wearing a dinner jacket or tuxedo:

- Socks. Black.
- Shoes. Black. Shiny and plain toe.
- Trousers. Black.
- Cummerbund. A soft fabric, belt-like wrap, which encircles the waist and is secured at the back. Your choice of color.
- Shirt. White and perhaps, pleated or tucked.
- Bow tie. Black obviously conforms to the "black tie" request, however, other dark colors are acceptable (e.g., burgundy, navy). The bow-tie color complements the jacket or cummerbund.
- Tuxedo or dinner jacket. Single- or double-breasted jacket (without tails). You may choose black or midnight blue, and in summer a white dinner jacket. (Bolder fabric colors come and go with fashion trends.)
- Accessories. Braces can be worn with a cummerbund and colors should coordinate. Cuff links for the shirt cuffs and studs (worn in place of buttons on formal shirts) should be made of precious metals (e.g., silver, gold). The pocket square, made of linen or silk in colors that coordinate with the tie or cummerbund, is tucked into the left breast pocket (not to extend more than an inch above the pocket). A waistcoat or vest may be worn in place of a cummerbund to cover the trouser waistband, and its color coordinates with the bow tie.

Although your options are narrow, be aware that your choices shouldn't be made haphazardly since they enhance or detract from your personal appearance. Your height, weight, and physical characteristics, must be considered as you make selections so that the result is flattering.

Everyday Business Etiquette puts the spotlight on the importance of "black-tie" correctness. This book is not, however, a fashion guide. In addition to the resources already mentioned, (e.g., formal-wear sales representatives), you may want to engage the services of an image consultant in preparing for a special black-tie business function. Remember, too, that fashions and accessories are influenced by times and locations. In the Southwest, for example, a Western-style tuxedo may be worn. This outfit may not be considered acceptable in other locales.

Toasts

A toastmaster or a company official may take charge of making a toast at a black-tie event. Generally speaking, the host makes the first toast. If you will make a toast or are likely to have to respond to a toast, you'll be able to be eloquent and appear more poised if you've prepared. By the way, it's not a breach of etiquette to merely lift a glass of champagne or other beverage to your lips when toasting an individual. Don't feel compelled to imbibe.

Toasts are generally offered at the end of a meal and before any speeches begin, and everyone but the person being toasted is expected to rise. If you are that person, rise after the tribute has been completed to say thank you. You may want to embellish your words of thanks with some brief comments but all that is necessary is a polite "thank you."

How You Feel

A toast should express your feelings. If it can be both clever and sincere your audience should take delight in your comments and the person to whom you're extending the toast should feel masterfully complimented.

A one- or two-minute salute is welcome, but a toast that runs three minutes or more qualifies as a speech and is neither proper nor welcome.

If someone makes a toast you think is clever, jot it down and save it. If you come across a notable statement when reading a book or newspaper, file it away. Browse library or book stores' shelves for books devoted to toasts. In other words, you don't have to invent something new. Do, however, take care to commit your chosen remarks to memory since you won't appear polished if you read from notes in order to deliver the toast.

If you use someone's business title when you rise to make a toast, be sure you know the correct title. If, for example, Marie Johns is Sales Director of the Northeast Region but she's also a company vice president, you'll want to announce her complete title. "I'd like to propose a toast to Marie Johns, Vice President, and Sales Director, Northeast Region. Ms. Johns, Marie, . . ."

If you omit someone's full title, you risk diminishing the person's importance and therefore, the tribute. Pronounce the person's name correctly, too. If you're not attentive to these details, your toast can achieve the opposite effect of what you intended and the individual may feel slighted.

A Graceful Exit

Don't be the last one to say good night.

Whether you attend a black-tie function at someone's home or estate, a major resort, a convention center, or a fine hotel, saying good night to your host, hostess, or important business associates at just the right moment can serve you well. It provides you an opportunity to share a quiet moment with any of these important people, as opposed to feeling rushed because others are bidding farewell, too. It's not easy to appear graceful while being propelled along with the crowd!

- If thanks are appropriate, extend your thanks.
- If good wishes are appropriate, extend your good wishes.
- If a compliment is appropriate, offer it.
- And, then, be on your way.

ON-THE-CAREER-PATH TIPS

- Read Chapter One: When High-Level Business Deals Call for High-Society Know-How
- Read Chapter Three: Dining-Table Etiquette You Didn't Learn at Home
- Read Chapter Six: At-the-Podium Protocol
- Read Chapter Ten: Introductions

STRATEGY YOU CAN USE

When you dress for the occasion—remember to slip into a festive state of mind, too. No matter what your job title, when you attend the function, you're a sales person! Vow to make everyone you meet and greet a little richer for the encounter.

2

The Finer Points of Interview Etiquette

An interview is an unvarnished getting-to-know-you session. Direct questions are not only allowed, they're expected. Whether you're asking most of the questions or providing most of the answers, you're making a statement. Your grasp of business etiquette will support you as you strive to reach your goal.

A popular book for children asks, "What can be the use of manners?" Young readers are informed "They make you a nice person to know."

As you work to obtain a job offer, or work to convince a job candidate to accept an offer, you advance your position if your manners make you a nice person to know.

DO'S & DON'TS THAT APPLY WHEN YOU INTERVIEW OTHERS

An interviewer who assumes that he or she is superior to the individual seated on the other side of the desk makes a mistake. Although you have decision-making power and the other person's chance of getting the job is somewhat dependent on your assessment, you'll perform better if you concentrate on your performance, not your status.

It's difficult to be a nice person to know when you view yourself as a superior person—someone who feels superior to others is inclined to dispense with niceties.

A List of Do's

- *Introduce yourself to the interviewee.* One highly qualified job candidate asked an interviewer who he was when the man began to fire questions at her without first identifying himself. This awkward beginning could have been avoided. It's courteous to rise and greet the job candidate by name and announce your name and position.

"Sally Jones, I'm Sarah Rathbay, Director of Human Resources. Please be seated."

"Mark Smith, I'm Brenda Briar, Administrative Assistant to the Vice President of Marketing. Make yourself comfortable."

- *Listen carefully.* A supervisor had worked hard on her interview technique and was so focused on asking questions in a particular order, she didn't listen carefully to answers. Two job candidates were of special interest to her boss, and when the supervisor was asked to compare their interview performances, she was on shaky ground.

  Listen carefully not only because it's the polite thing to do but because it enables you to utilize new information. A person's response may prompt you to ask a related question that reveals even more about this candidate's suitability for the position.

- *Say what you mean.* Three job candidates met with the vice president who would make the final hiring decision. Since many of his questions were ambiguous, each candidate interpreted them differently and answered accordingly. (Had any of the candidates been in a less stressful setting, they might have asked for clarification.) As a result, the vice president couldn't intelligently compare responses and wasn't in a strong position to make a decision.

  Can an interviewee understand your question? Should one question be shaped into two questions for the sake of clarity? Clear communication promotes cooperation and when you remove communication stumbling blocks you're less likely to waste time. Showing respect for another person's time is an important aspect of business etiquette.

- *Act decisively.* A talented designer felt so buoyed by the rapport she and the president of a major art design company established during her interview, she made inquiry about renting an apartment near the company's offices. When five days passed and she didn't get any feedback, she decided she'd better get her job search back into high gear. When the call finally came to notify her the job was hers, she hesitated. The long delay suggested to her that management was slow to make decisions.

  It's comfortable to work with people who don't sit on the fence too long weighing their "should I's?" Being decisive is definitely an attribute associated with well-mannered people. Consider, for example, how it appears to a hostess who passes a plate of fried chicken to you while you prod several portions with the serving fork before making a selection. "Is something wrong?" the hostess asks herself. "Is he always like this?"

The job candidate wonders, too.

A List of Don'ts

- *Don't keep someone waiting.* It's rude.
- *Don't mispronounce the interviewee's name.* Be gracious if an individual corrects you because you mispronounce his or her name. If it's a name with an unusual spelling, start off by asking, "Am I pronouncing Jameesour, correctly?" If you're told, "It's pronounced Jamswa," devise a clever way to remember. It's permissible to scribble a note to yourself with a phonetic clue (e.g., Jams-wa) and then unobtrusively refer to that note as needed. If you can't handle a simple task like a name pronunciation, this interviewee has every right to wonder how well you handle the larger job of representing the company and why the company gives you an opportunity to do so.
- *Don't sidestep questions.* It's impolite to ignore a question. If you can't answer, say so. If you don't wish to answer, acknowledge that you're not at liberty to divulge information. If you prefer to answer later, say that you will and don't forget to do so. As a matter of fact, if you think a candidate has potential, solicit questions. "Is there anything you'd like to ask me?"
- *Don't permit interruptions.* It's courteous to give someone your undivided attention when you and he or she have agreed to a specific meeting time. Don't accept routine calls from others or permit anyone to enter your offices to divert you from your objective. Your signature on correspondence or purchase orders can wait until later.
- *Don't neglect to clearly signal the end of the interview.* Rise and thank the individual for coming. That makes it clear the session is over. If you sit at your desk thumbing through papers or you repeatedly glance at your watch, the interviewee may feel as though you're sending exit hints. He or she will find it difficult to concentrate on the conversation if it seems like the time to leave and you won't benefit from the exchange. Let the person know what's next, too. "We'll be interviewing people for this position for the next four days. Sometimes management requests a second interview and that can be a week or more away depending on

whether key executives are available. You may not hear further for another ten days, but be assured, all job applicants are notified one way or the other."

Your considerate conclusion sends interviewees away feeling good about the company. Not everyone will be hired but everyone has the potential for being a customer or client or perhaps an employee at some future time.

There's nothing sacrosanct about the illustrations noted above. You can substitute a completely different set of illustrations which support different mandates. Examples are intended to demonstrate how performance is bolstered when you practice the fine art of business etiquette.

What the Law Dictates

Some questions are forbidden by federal, state or local laws. You may or may not agree with the wisdom of these edicts but you must comply or the company is liable to be penalized.

Rely on the company's legal advisors for periodic updates because laws change constantly in this area.

The rules target job bias, and you must stay away from questions which may be considered discriminatory. This is easier said than done since it's sometimes difficult to know precisely where you may not tread.

It doesn't help if you politely ask a job candidate's age, since that's a no-no. You may mask your surprise when an applicant arrives in a wheelchair and tactfully inquire whether or not he's permanently disabled, but when you do so, you're violating the law. In other words, your mastery of good manners won't help you when it's mastery of the law that's of paramount importance.

Experts recommend questions be framed on printed applications or during interviews to glean answers that help determine if someone has the skills and experience to do the job. Period.

The following currently fall into the *don't ask* category:

- Whether or not a person has the responsibility for caring for young children
- A birth date, unless there are special circumstances (because age discrimination may be suggested)
- Whether the individual has ever been arrested (although it's generally permissible to inquire whether an individual has been convicted of a crime)

- Whether an individual has AIDS or is HIV-positive
- About smoking habits. In many states, you can't ask. You probably can ask whether the candidate can comply with the company's no-smoking policy.

HOW BEST TO PRESENT YOURSELF TO GET THE JOB

"It is a very great thing to be able to think as you like; but, after all, an important question remains: what *you think."*

Matthew Arnold (*Democracy*, 1861)

You convey what you think in a variety of ways. You're not communicating solely with words.

Some experts say you must dress for success by opting for clothing and grooming practices which make you look as though you're already doing the job you aspire to do.

This strategy helps to tell others what you think.

The message? "I think I can do the job I aspire to."

Messages are also sent with:

- good posture
- a firm handshake
- a confident stride
- a calm exterior (i.e., hands folded in your lap as opposed to hands fidgeting with papers or clothing)

It's important to be aware of all the tools at your disposal so that you're thoroughly prepared to win a job offer.

- Can you interact successfully with others who are formal, conventional, reserved, proper?
- Can you put a lid on your own reserved manner when others behave in a casual and unconventional way?
- Do you gravitate towards people who know when to behave in a prim and proper manner and when to relax some of the rules?

Most people fit into one of these categories.

Your own behavior supports you as you tell others what you think about yourself as a job candidate.

Example: The job is in corporate communications. The real estate management company has been in business for ninety years. You know the company image is staid, honorable, aloof, but modern. Many company clients are middle-aged. You just celebrated your thirtieth birthday and tend to be gregarious and outgoing. You know you can do the job and you want it. In addition to dressing in a conservative fashion, you adopt a formal demeanor. You:

- Ask permission to ask questions instead of just "firing away."
- Put your briefcase on the floor next to your chair. Wait to be asked to produce writing samples and say, "excuse me" when you look away to reach for your briefcase and produce these materials. (In a less formal setting, you might put the briefcase on your lap and retrieve samples for the interviewer without waiting to be asked to do so.)
- Sit back in your chair and wait quietly, comfortable to be doing nothing but wait, when the interviewer accepts a telephone call.
- Rise when another person enters the room. (Ordinarily, you'd remain seated until an introduction to a new arrival appears to be imminent.)

Example: The management job is in automobile rentals at a busy airport. You've spent the last six years managing a fine linen supply shop located in a fashionable part of town. You're soft-spoken and work at a leisurely pace. You're looking for a change as well as increased income and know you have the skills to succeed in this position. In addition to selecting a sports jacket and slacks instead of a suit, you accessorize with a brightly colored tie. You:

- Walk into the room at a brisk pace and introduce yourself without delay. (Ordinarily, you might proceed into the room at a slower pace and wait for the interviewer to get things started.)
- Accept the interviewer's offer of a cup of coffee instead of demurring.
- Ask one or two questions when there's a lull in the conversation without asking for permission to do so.

This engineering of your demeanor to fit the situation tells them "I think I fit-in nicely here."

Something else happens when you adopt the style you perceive to be correct in this potential new job environment: you feel right. When you feel right, it's easier to "do" right!

Preparing for a Second Interview

An advertising executive found himself at odds with the editor-in-chief of a magazine who was intent on making sweeping editorial changes. "We sold thousands of subscriptions to folks based on what we told them to expect. You've got to deliver what we sold."

The same goes for you. You'll have to repeat your previous performance. Whatever you did to get yourself invited back, do it again.

If possible, wear different clothing but keep your look the same.

MANNERS THAT TARGET A CLOSED-DOOR OFFICE INTERVIEW

You may be talking to one or more interviewers and taking questions from one or more interviewers. The setting supports a serious down-to-business attitude. Don't be fooled into thinking something special is needed. As a matter of fact, some interviewers like to see how a job candidate responds when he or she feels "squeezed." Handle this interview session the same way you'll handle any interview. Keep your eye on your goal and respond accordingly.

SHOW-OFF MANNERS FOR A MEAL-TIME INTERVIEW

A meal-time interview that's announced is a rare thing since most people agree that a comprehensive question-and-answer session doesn't complement good food. Still, a breakfast, lunch, or dinner invitation extended for the purpose of getting to know you better is nothing short of an interview. Use it to showcase the you that can't be introduced in a printed résumé.

Unless you're sure that your table manners are perfect, you may want to prepare yourself for the meal-time interview by having a trial meal at a fine restaurant. If it will be a breakfast meeting, make it a breakfast meal. Observe the other diners in action and note both attractive and inappropriate behavior. If you dine alone, it's rather easy to accomplish this goal without appearing to be a "spy."

> *"All things are filled full of signs, and it is a wise man who can learn about one thing from another."*
>
> Plotinus (205–270 A.D.)

Here are some pointers:

- Don't groom yourself at the table.

- Your napkin belongs in your lap throughout the meal. If you must leave the table briefly, place the napkin on your chair as a signal to the server that you will return.
- Feet should be on the floor in front of you as opposed to at the sides of your chair or with a foot dangling while your knees are crossed.
- Don't toy with utensils and don't gesture or make your point using china or goblets. Salt and pepper shakers, for example, have been used by job candidates to represent everything from the customer to the competition.
- Don't put your elbows in your ear and don't put them on the table either.
- If a utensil or napkin drops, ask your server to supply you with another.
- Don't wave to someone you know. If the individual makes eye contact with you, nod your head and smile, then focus your attention on people at your own table.
- If it's not finger food, don't treat it as such. This practice has become more commonplace with the advent of fast-food emporiums. Fried potatoes should be lifted with a fork, not the fingers. The same is true for bacon strips and melon slices. Break your bread, toast, or roll into smaller pieces and consume only a small portion at a time. If you spread butter or jam on these baked goods, add it to the small portions, one at a time. (In other words, don't coat a large piece of toast with jam and then proceed to break it up.)
- Use serving utensils for serving and return them to their original place. Don't substitute your table utensils for serving pieces.
- Don't offer or accept food from another's plate. "This is so delicious, you must taste it," isn't appropriate at a business meal.

If you have questions about how to eat any particular food, find out before the meal-time interview, or don't order that food.

You'll learn a lot by being a casual observer. Be mindful, however, that the prominent executive dining with you may not have fine table manners. If that's the case, take care not to mimic his or her performance.

What was it Plotinus said so long ago? It bears repeating: "All things are filled full of signs, and it is a wise man who can learn about one thing from another."

Assume the interviewer embraces this philosophy, too. Your impeccable table manners support a positive learning experience for the interviewer and bode well for you and your chances for a job offer.

By the way, there's no reason to reserve your best manners only for special occasions. Use them all the time and they won't atrophy.

COMPORTMENT WHEN YOU MEET IN AN ATYPICAL SETTING

It's not unusual for human resource personnel to meet job candidates on college campuses, at job fairs held in convention centers, or at booths set up in shopping malls. If the encounter is unscheduled, you won't be dressed for the occasion and may have to work harder to look as though you're an excellent job candidate. Even when the interview has been scheduled, the fish-out-of-the-water environment can work counter to your purpose.

To make a good impression, trade your leisurely gait for a purposeful stride, sit back in your chair and place your feet on the floor in front of you, and tune out noises and distractions that are not a usual part of a job interview setting. This is one time the advice, "When in Rome, do as the Romans do" doesn't apply. Disregard the setting. Do as you would do if you were being interviewed in a more business-like setting. Your command of business etiquette helps enhance your image. Be attentive, don't interrupt the interviewer, and use the person's name as you speak, making sure to pronounce it correctly.

If this meeting is successful, it should be followed by a more traditional meeting. Use this occasion to learn as much about the company and job opportunity as possible. If you aren't favorably impressed, you may not want another meeting.

SIX COURTEOUS REJOINDERS WHEN SAVOIR FAIRE IS LACKING

(1) "Don't call us, we'll call you," sounds like a brush-off. Still, if an interviewer leaves you with those words, don't jump to conclusions. Make your exit gracefully or ask, "Do you expect to make a decision this week or next week?" This question is like the old egg-cream question. A soda fountain clerk knew he'd earn a nickel for every egg he sold to customers who ordered this regional favorite. He didn't have any success by asking, "Would you like an egg in your egg cream?" He did a brisk business, however, when he phrased his question, "One egg or two?"

If you're going to adopt a wait and see attitude, fine. If you want to learn more, however, make certain you phrase your question so the answer can't be vague. A skilled interviewer would be more considerate and leave you better informed.

(2) You're the interviewer, dining with a job candidate. A colleague comes to your table to introduce a friend. You rise to greet them and introduce the job

candidate. Your colleague engages the candidate in conversation you feel is inappropriate: "Josh is a tough taskmaster! Take care, young man." "I think I hear a Southern accent. Am I correct?" Moreover, neither he nor his friend seem inclined to leave. The four of you are standing and talking and people at nearby tables are glancing your way.

You ask the job candidate to be seated and say to the visitors, "It was good to meet you, Marie. I'll let you and John get on to your table." "John, I'll call you Friday so we can talk further." You then take your seat and make eye contact with your guest. You have, in fact, told the visitors where to go! Still, you were polite.

It's not reasonable to linger at someone's restaurant table when they're engaged in a business discussion. It's totally inappropriate to make comments to someone's business guest which could be construed as too familiar.

(3) You ask your boss to step into your office to meet a job candidate. The individual's résumé and references are impressive and you know your boss is eager to fill the position. When she arrives, the interviewee remains seated and casts her eyes downward. Your boss takes a seat nearby and asks the candidate, "Has Sarah told you our company is expanding and we have many new projects on the horizon?" "Yeah," says your candidate. After a few more monosyllabic replies, your boss makes an exit. You ask the candidate if something is troubling her. "Your boss looks like my stepmother and I hate my stepmother," is the response. You immediately but courteously dismiss this individual. "I wish you well as you continue your job search," you say as you walk her to the door.

Apparently you've unmasked a troubled individual. It's appropriate to dismiss her without delay and make it clear there's no job for her at your company. You'll want to apprise your boss of the situation and let her know you're sorry you didn't detect the problem before she became involved.

(4) The job candidate whips out a cigarette and plops down on your sofa. "It's sure nice to be in a private office," he remarks. "So many of the public buildings in this city are off limits to smokers. By the way, I hope you don't mind if I smoke." He takes a deep drag and smoke billows into your office.

The fact is, you do mind. "Ray, our employee lounge is at the end of the corridor and you can smoke your cigarette there. If you want to take five minutes in the lounge, that's fine. I'll ask the receptionist to show you the way."

Most people recognize that smoking is a serious addiction. Ray is job hunting and probably feeling more stress than usual. He now knows he can't smoke in your office but your courteous accommodation of his needs puts you both back on a level playing field. It may be that Ray is going to be the person you decide to hire and he may have a long and successful career with the company.

(5) You're being interviewed and can hardly believe your ears because the interviewer is saying negative things about the company. "This company claims to be an equal-opportunity employer, but let me tell you, the starting salary isn't even close to what other employers in this town offer. Are you able to accept a low-paying job and stay with it for the first year? Management here takes the view that if an employee can't be loyal to the company for at least one year, he or she doesn't deserve a raise."

Recognize that what sounds negative may only be revealing. Moreover, it may be part of a plan to test the mettle of interviewees. Still, if negative comments are forthcoming, you need only listen without comment. In this case, you've been asked a question and you answer, "I'd be honored to receive a job offer." Or, "I understand there's room for growth here."

On the chance the interviewer is out of line, your limited response or positive comments permit her to get back on track with ease. If you expound on the company's faults and embellish the interviewer's comments, she may suddenly regret her lapse in good judgment and banish you out of embarrassment.

(6) During your interview, an important customer knocks on the door. You are introduced and the interview comes to a halt so the interviewer can tend to the customer. Fifteen minutes later, you realize that if you're kept waiting much longer, you'll probably miss a train and be late for a special family gathering. When you attempt to interrupt, the interviewer says, "I'll be with you in a minute, Jones." Ten minutes pass and you rise and say, "Excuse me, gentlemen, I have another appointment. May I call tomorrow to make a new appointment with you to complete our interview?"

The interviewer waves you off. "I'll just need a minute, Jones. Keep your seat."

If you do, you risk missing your next appointment. You'll exit at your peril, but exit you probably should. "Mr. Appleton, I don't have a choice but to call again. Thanks for your time and I'll show myself out." Your courteous but firm actions speak louder than words. If Appleton ultimately offers you a job, he knows you're not easily intimidated. If you accept a job with Mr. Appleton, you know he may not be considerate of people he views as subordinates. First impressions are worthy of consideration.

MAINTAINING GRACE UNDER FIRE

> *"If a man be gracious and courteous to strangers, it shows he is a citizen of the world, and that his heart is no island cut off from other lands, but a continent that joins to them."*
>
> Francis Bacon (*"Of Goodness and Goodness of Nature"*)

You and your interviewer are probably strangers to one another and have no reason to quarrel. Still, during the interview process some questions and comments may make you feel uncomfortable.

"So you weren't smart enough to win a scholarship to the university. Most of our recent employees were scholarship recipients. Do you think you can fit in here?"

"I can tell from your address you come from a Republican neighborhood. We tend to be Republicans in this office and I'm sure you'll fit in should we decide to offer you this job."

"I see you worked for T & T Manufacturing. They don't run a modern operation, so I imagine you're not acquainted with Total Quality Management practices."

It's easier to demonstrate personal polish and poise when the interview doesn't push into treacherous territory. It's not so easy to maintain grace if you must defend yourself, or if you believe your silence suggests you agree with preposterous comments.

The person who is provocative may have excellent motives but there's neither time nor sufficient information to interpret motives. You can only take charge of your own responses. Since your goal is to ace the interview, you're well advised to remember Francis Bacon's words. If your interviewer is trying to shake you up to see how you react, you demonstrate a command of yourself and the bigger picture when you act in a gracious and courteous manner. If he or she is a fool, you maintain your standards by remaining polite.

Later, if and when you have a job offer, you may decide this "under fire" maneuver was sufficiently objectionable or the interviewer so representative of the company, that you decide to say "no."

EIGHTEEN UNMENTIONABLES: WHAT NOT TO SAY AT AN INTERVIEW

Here are eighteen topics or conversational gambits that the job seeker must avoid:

1. *Proprietary information regarding your former employer. Not only is this wrong, it suggests to the interviewer you aren't trustworthy.*
2. *Horror stories about your recent divorce. Even if everything you say is accurate, the topic suggests you're indiscreet.*
3. *Feelings you harbor which could be considered sexist or racist. You may think the interviewer shares your opinion, but you're treading on thin ice. Sexist and racist views don't belong in the workplace.*
4. *Politics*
5. *Religion*
6. *Favorite sports team or sports figure. You may favor one the interviewer opposes. Although it would be irrational for him or her to hold that against you, it can happen.*
7. *Your children or grandchildren—when it comes to bragging. Your pocket full of photographs of the little ones is out of place even if the interviewer has photographs of his or her family on display.*
8. *An offer to get something or do something special for the interviewer. "I can get it for you wholesale," for example, may be both accurate and considerate in a different setting. Here, it's out of place and may appear to be a bribe.*
9. *How terrible the weather is or how horrible the traffic is or anything that's especially negative about the place you just vacated. (You may be criticizing the interviewer's hometown of which he or she is especially fond.)*
10. *How much you dislike mathematics or science or any particular pursuit that may seem unrelated to the job you're seeking. (Management at this company may prefer that all employees be proficient in math or science.)*
11. *Personal dislikes that don't advance your position. If, for example, you mention you'd certainly dye your hair another color if you were born a*

redhead, you may discover the CEO of this company has flaming red hair. Of course, if you say you are always punctual and are distressed with individuals who are tardy, you're probably on safe ground.

12. *Complaints about being kept waiting or how hot it is in the room where you filled out a job application or took a typing test. Complaints don't support the flow of positive information you want to deliver to the interviewer.*
13. *Don't be a name-dropper. If, for example, your former boss was a home decorator and you assisted when she decorated the home of a famous person, reporting the goings-on there isn't worthy of mention. If you're actually on friendly terms with famous people, take care not to make it appear that you're boasting.*
14. *Reveal all the things you won't do. If, for example, you can't agree to stay after five because of responsibilities at home, there's no need to volunteer this information. An exception to this strategy would be if the employer stated it was necessary to work late, on occasion. If that's an integral part of this job description, be truthful. Remember, some no-can-do circumstances change and you may be in a different position should you eventually be confronted with a specific request.*
15. *Anything that pops into your head to fill a silence. Think before you speak.*
16. *Pointless chatter. Once you answer a question or make a comment, stop. It serves no useful purpose to say too much.*
17. *Lavish praise for the person conducting the interview. Even when you're truly impressed by this individual, praise may be misunderstood under these circumstances. You can, of course, say, "I enjoyed meeting you. Thank you."*
18. *Negative body language. Don't slump in your chair, groom your hair or nails, or slip out of your shoes.*

You'll probably be able to add to this list as you travel the interview circuit. Make notes. Remember to glance at the list before you keep your next appointment for an interview.

Happy hunting!

3

Dining-Table Etiquette You Didn't Learn at Home

When you're dining with business associates, you should be more calculating than when you're dining with family and friends. Recognize that a business get-together isn't a forum designed for frolicking. Moreover, breaking bread with business associates isn't done simply for pleasure.

You want something!

A sale. A job. A promotion. A lead. A confirmation. Cooperation.

Although the following pointers may serve you well whenever you dine, they spotlight the business dining scene.

If you feel the need to brush up on your table manners, read Craig Claiborne's *Elements of Etiquette—A Guide to Table Manners in an Imperfect World* (NY: William Morrow, 1992). Another helpful book is *The Rituals of Dinner: The Origins, Evolution, Eccentricities, and Meaning of Table Manners* by Margaret Visser (NY: Grove Weidenfeld, 1991).

WHAT YOU SHOULD CONSIDER BEFORE ORDERING

- Don't order foods you don't feel comfortable about when it comes down to eating techniques. If you tend to slurp your pasta, for example, and don't feel you'll be successful twirling it onto your fork with the aid of a large spoon, order rice!

- Avoid foods that may stain or get caught in your teeth. It's difficult to look suave and knowledgeable when several of your front teeth are wrapped in spinach greens.

- When the menu doesn't mention whether or not the fish is served boneless, inquire. Choking on bones or delicately putting your fingers into your mouth to retrieve them can be a real show stopper.
- If you're not sure whether or not the fried chicken may be eaten without benefit of fork and knife, select something else from the menu that is clearly not finger food. If you choose chicken cordon bleu, watch out for melted-cheese strings that tend to dangle after you take a bite.
- If you're dining with a vegetarian, you might want to order a vegetarian dish, too. This is especially considerate if only two of you are dining. An entree which comes complete with a head (e.g., some fish or fowl) may prove especially disquieting to your vegetarian associate.

A guest who has special dietary considerations based upon ethical or religious beliefs may be thoroughly relieved if you avoid ordering proscribed dishes.

None of the above pointers are rules of business etiquette. They are, however, examples of good judgment. Good judgment is at the core of *Everyday Business Etiquette* techniques.

In Roger E. Axtell's book, *Do's and Taboos of Hosting International Visitors* (NY: John Wiley, 1990), he mentions that people in the United States often eat a light lunch while business guests from overseas usually prefer a large meal midday and would select a later hour to dine than our customary noon time slot.

Obviously, inviting someone to enjoy a light meal with you at noon isn't breaking any rules of business etiquette. It could, however, be viewed as an example of poor judgment.

Again, be prepared. Find out what's comfortable for those with whom you're planning to break bread.

At Home

When you were growing up, it's not likely that your elders were confronted with so many variables and, therefore, not likely they passed all the appropriate words of wisdom down to you.

Even when you believe you were the recipient of the very best dining-table training, be aware that your counterparts in other locales may have received a slightly different education.

Axtell advises that while your mother told you you could keep one hand in your lap while eating, German mothers instructed their offspring to keep their hands in view above the table at all times.

He also mentions that many foods eaten in this country may be repulsive to foreign visitors (e.g., marshmallows, white bread), and vice versa. In South Korea, dog meat is served while sheep's eyeballs are on the menu in Saudi Arabia.

These preferences may or may not disturb you, but once you tune in to how others may respond you'll want to take measures that will favorably influence the business dining experience.

Remember, too, that by now many people have gained a great deal of experience working with people from different cultures and backgrounds. Therefore, the individual you're planning to dine with may conform to customs prevalent in the environment in which you both find yourselves conducting business.

Be aware of possible differences. Be sensitive to an individual's needs. But, assume nothing. When you adapt that credo, you're practically ready to order!

THE A–Z SCOOP ON ALCOHOLIC BEVERAGES

One of the things you'll want to do at a business meal is keep your voice moderate to low in pitch. Have you ever noticed how folks who have a few alcoholic beverages can rarely do that?

It's not the most obvious reason for having no more than one alcoholic beverage with a business meal but it's worthy of note.

If you indulge in too much wine, beer or mixed drinks, you become suspect to an observant companion. Suspect of what?

Not being in control. Not being trustworthy. Not exercising good judgment.

These are not messages you want to send. When you make every effort to practice proper business etiquette, it doesn't make sense to risk all by drinking too much.

A good rule of thumb is no more than one.

Of course, you needn't have any alcoholic beverages. In today's business climate, this choice is not unusual. Moreover, if someone opts for fruit juice or a soft drink, don't comment on the selection. Don't press any individual to accept an alcoholic beverage. It's not a prerequisite for conducting business. Moreover, many people don't consume alcohol for health or religious reasons, or both.

Wine, Please

Whether or not you choose to drink an alcoholic beverage, you may find yourself in the position of selecting one or more bottles of wine for your guests.

If you're a wine connoisseur, you need no help in making your choice. You may, however, not be at liberty to expend too many dollars on a selection. If your company is paying for the meal, it's both sensible and necessary to be mindful of expense. Still, if you know your guests are wine aficionados, you may want to splurge.

Do some advance planning. Let your boss know you anticipate a more costly entertainment tab than usual. Confer with the wine steward or the maitre d' ahead of time to ascertain which wines are available. Don't hesitate to ask which wines are currently favored by patrons who appreciate fine wines. Armed with this information, you should be able to make selections that are beyond reproach.

Consider, too, that some wine lovers prefer to savor fine wines when they're relaxed and able to take time to appreciate the wine's qualities. The business meal may not be the time for such wine.

If you're not a wine connoisseur, you can invite someone in your party to make selections or turn to the wine steward for direction. As a general rule, don't choose the least expensive wines on the list. Today, the old rules about red wine with red meat, white wine with fish and fowl, are held inviolate by some but disregarded by others. Wait until people order before making a selection. Determine which wine will complement the food selections and announce your choices to those assembled. Ask if that meets with everyone's approval. Listen carefully to responses and adjust your order if necessary. Or, if you prefer, order both red and white wines to be brought to the table. It's generally acceptable to order a glass of wine, too, and that may suffice when one individual prefers a dish that requires a different wine than the rest.

Sip the sample of wine that's offered to you as host. Your task here is to make sure it hasn't deteriorated. Too much exposure to air, for example, causes wine to become vinegar-like. This happens when the bottle's cork doesn't fit tightly. If you believe the bottle of wine isn't good, quietly inform the wine steward. Don't turn your disapproval into a showy affair. This business meal is not an opportunity to demonstrate your facility with wine. At the same time, you don't want your guests to be served something that won't taste good.

If the wine steward tastes the wine and disagrees with you, be prepared to stand your ground. Business associates know you to be a strong and capable individual. Don't permit this episode to undermine the image you've worked hard to establish.

Too Much of a Good Thing

An anonymous shanty you may know asks:

"What shall we do with the drunken sailor, early in the morning?"

It's not an easy question to answer, whether you're dealing with a sailor or an executive and whether it's morning, noon, or night.

A cardinal rule is never let someone drive an automobile when there's any doubt regarding the person's sobriety.

If you believe that someone at the dinner meeting has become intoxicated, be tactful but be insistent that the individual is not permitted to navigate from the restaurant or meeting place to the next destination.

Sometimes it's difficult to judge if someone has had too much to drink. Moreover, you may be aware that the individual has only ordered one drink and you therefore question your assessment. Be aware that under some circumstances one drink may render someone impaired. Moreover, the individual may have been drinking alcoholic beverages prior to his or her arrival at the restaurant.

If the meal-time meeting hasn't concluded, and after-dinner drinks are served (e.g., Port, Cognac), don't permit the intoxicated individual to be served more alcohol. Countermand his or her order, if necessary, and ask that coffee be served.

You're not expected to be this individual's keeper but you can look out for his or her safety and safeguard your company, too. Today, the line of responsibility is long when it comes to answering for the actions of someone who, while intoxicated, harms other people or damages property.

Be discreet and don't discuss this individual's tipsy behavior in the future. It can serve no useful purpose.

HOW TO ARRANGE SEATING TO YOUR ADVANTAGE

Determine which position at the dining table will best advance your goals.

One young executive liked to sit directly across the table from a key client. She had noticed the man had difficulty hearing and guessed he was a lip-reader. She knew that other luncheon attendees would vie to sit on either side of him, but she had the favored position when seated directly across from him.

A purchasing agent disliked being seated between suppliers because he was always turning his head to listen or to address one person while turning his back to the other. He preferred the end seat at the table to avoid this awkward position.

The chairman of the board of a major corporation preferred a head-of-the-table position whether he was the host or an invited guest at a meal-time gathering. Privately, he believed this seat of honor enhanced his image and made him appear powerful. As a result, he coveted this spot at the table and would direct his secretary to call ahead and find out where he was to be seated. If he couldn't sit where he preferred, he sometimes didn't attend.

Here are some ways to manipulate seating arrangements to your advantage:

- Call ahead and ask that you be escorted to the place of your choice at the table when you arrive. Be prepared to discreetly thank the dining-room host or hostess with a gratuity.
- Arrive early and take your place at the table ahead of the others. Order a beverage while you wait. It's less likely you'll be asked to change your place after you've staked it out with your beverage.
- Don't be the last to arrive unless you're prepared to accept the only available seat at the table.
- Ask a colleague to change places with you.

WHERE TO WAIT IF YOU ARRIVE FIRST AND OTHER POINTERS

(1) It's courteous to rise and greet other attendees when they approach the table. If you'd prefer to avoid this ritual, don't arrive at the table early.

(2) *Can I use a toothpick while seated at the table?*

No. It may, however, be customary to do so in some places. (Roger Axtell claims it's not an uncommon practice in the Orient.)

(3) *I know that it's not polite to freshen my makeup at the table but can I do so if I'm quick about it?*

No. It's inappropriate and many attribute such behavior to a lack of manners.

(4) *I don't like to talk when I eat because I swallow too much air. Can I sit quietly while I eat or will others find this standoffish?*

You needn't originate conversation while you chew but you may have to respond to a question or someone's attempt to engage you in conversation. If need be, leave your fork on your dinner plate and let conversation reign.

(5) *If my food isn't acceptable, should I send it back or suffer in silence?*

It's one thing to avoid a commotion but quite another to stay silent and suffer. Don't! Direct the server how to proceed. Be clear about what you expect, and be polite. "This cream sauce is too salty for me. Please take it back to the kitchen and bring the menu. I'll make a different selection."

(6) *Is it necessary to "small talk" or can I get right down to business?*

Small talk is an important preamble to business, so come prepared to chat. Some people may not be willing to discuss business until the meal is finished and coffee is served. They may consider you rude if you attempt to do otherwise.

As a matter of fact, perhaps you are one of those people! Make your preferences known unless you have virtually no choice in the matter. Ask about the agenda before you set a date to dine. Perhaps a meeting around the conference table is more appropriate.

(7) *How should I respond if someone gossips and doesn't hesitate to mention names of colleagues in this public place?*

Respond in the same way you would if this individual indulged in this kind of conversation at the water cooler, in the commuter van, or anywhere else. Don't cooperate. Lead the discussion in another direction. If the individual doesn't get the message, you may want to quietly remark that you don't indulge in office gossip. If the situation is out of control, make an excuse and exit as soon as possible.

(8) *What should I do if my dinner guest can't find anything to order on the menu?*

Don't hesitate to ask the server to bring something that's not listed. This request isn't as unusual as you may think because many people have special food regimens. If your guest can't be accommodated, you have no choice but to leave the establishment and find another place to dine.

(9) *Can I take my jacket off and put it on the back of my chair?*

No. Even when dining in a casual setting, this arrangement makes you look sloppy.

(10) *Can I tell my guest that he has spinach stuck on his teeth?*

Probably not. That is unless you can think of a way to signal him without making him feel foolish.

(11) *If I'm served hot food and others haven't been served yet, may I begin to eat?*

No. Wait until everyone is served before you start eating unless those with whom you're dining urge you not to wait.

(12) *What should I do if my beeper signals me to contact my office but the meal has just been served?*

The restaurant meeting may be more sacrosanct than an office meeting because people who are served hot or cold foods should be free to enjoy these dishes without delay. When you're distracted by a beeper tone, everyone is distracted. Make arrangements with your secretary or communication service so that you're not "beeped" in this time slot unless there's a clearly defined emergency.

(13) *Must I take my hat off in a restaurant?*

A woman may leave her hat on when she dines, since the hat is considered part of her outfit. A gentleman, on the other hand, is expected to remove his hat when he's indoors. There are exceptions. In the Southwest, for example, some men keep their Western-style hats on in restaurants and other indoor gathering places. Some people cover their heads at all times owing to religious practices. Prepare to follow customary guidelines yourself, but take note of local customs and expect some departures from traditional manners.

(14) *If my host has arranged for a table in the smoking section of the restaurant and I'm disturbed by smoke, can I request a change of tables?*

If only two of you are dining and you know your host reasonably well, by all means ask about changing locations. If your party consists of more than two, or if the establishment is very busy, another suitable table may not be available. It's best to request in advance that a table be reserved in the non-smoking section when you accept an invitation.

HOW TO HANDLE THE BILL

If you invite someone to dine you should be prepared to pay the bill. If only, it were that simple . . .

- If your guest insists that she's going to pay for her meal, it's not worth a tussle to dissuade her. Be gracious and split the bill.
- A junior executive invites his boss to lunch knowing they both have company credit cards and expense accounts, though the senior person has a larger expense account. If the senior executive reaches for the check, there's no need for the junior executive to protest.
- You invite a colleague to lunch and her husband is seated at a nearby table with his own guests. He stops at your table to greet his wife and tells you he's spoken to your server and made arrangements to take care of your bill. Thank him and tell him you'd like to return the favor. It's best to be gracious about such a gift even if you feel the man is overbearing and his takeover of the bill is inappropriate.
- If you want to avoid hassles about the check and you want to pay for the meals, arrange with restaurant personnel to settle the charges without bringing the check to the table. Make these arrangements when you call to make your reservation.
- If each person expects to purchase his or her own meal, notify the server you'll want separate checks when you place your orders.

WHEN TO GO AND WHEN TO STAY

There is life after the business meal. When you've accepted an invitation for breakfast or lunch, it's understood that each person will return to his or her workplace after the meal-time meeting. A dinner appointment, however, can leave you wondering: Should you go? Should you stay? How can you politely bring the meal to an end?

Moreover, as darkness falls, transportation and personal safety may become an issue. Trains and other transportation modes that operate at frequent intervals around 5:00 P.M. will probably operate less frequently by 8:00 P.M.

Taxi stands, bus stops, and train stations can be dark, lonely, and dangerous places after rush-hour crowds have departed. Consider your own and your dinner companion's circumstances.

If, however, travel considerations don't apply, you may still want to put a well-defined end to the dinner meeting. Here are some approaches:

- "I've got to read a forty-page controller's report before I retire, so I think you'll agree I'd better take my leave. Thank you for an enjoyable and productive session."
- "I think we've covered everything on our agenda. The hour grows late and we all deserve an opportunity to relax before this busy day draws to a close. Thank you for coming."
- "Ladies and gentlemen, I think it's time to relinquish this table to the establishment's staff. It looks as though we're the last to leave."

Rise when you bid your farewell and you'll be that much closer to making your exit. Don't be insensitive to the signals another person sends out when he or she wants to politely end a session.

HOW TO DEAL WITH AN UNINVITED INDIVIDUAL

Don't do anything to encourage the arrival of an uninvited party at your table. If an acquaintance approaches the table because she recognizes you, rise graciously, acknowledge her presence but make it clear you're unable to spend time with her.

"Good to see you, Helen. Let me telephone you tomorrow and we'll set a date to meet."

Don't introduce Helen to the others at the table and vice versa because such a courtesy sends the wrong message. You're not trying to include Helen in—you're attempting to fend her off, albeit in a courteous way.

If another person at the table is occupied with an uninvited individual and business conversation is delayed, you have little choice but to exercise patience. If the conversation drags on, however, you may want to announce that you have time constraints to consider and will have to leave soon. The person seated at the table may appreciate your intervention, especially if it has the desired effect and the uninvited individual leaves.

While you're thinking about ways to fend off an uninvited person, make a pact with yourself not to become the uninvited person. If you should pass by a table occupied by business acquaintances, stop briefly. Offer your greetings and move on.

ACCEPTABLE TOPICS OF MEAL-TIME DISCUSSION AND HANDLING RULE-BREAKERS

For purposes of maintaining dining-table etiquette, acceptable topics of discussion are those topics that don't offend anyone seated at the table.

If you notice, for example, that a client grows fidgety while your partner provides a detailed accounting of recent improvements in wastewater treatment plants, your partner's topic isn't acceptable.

When someone turns pale listening to a discussion of the gory aftermath of an automobile collision, that subject isn't acceptable.

Of course, being fidgety or turning pale are easy clues. Some people may be offended but exhibit no outward signs of distress.

Get into the habit of occasionally scanning the faces of those seated around the table. Be ready to act if you notice signs of distress.

One useful ploy is to change the subject.

Another is to discreetly signal the individual who is breaking the rules. A gentle nudge targeted at the person's shinbone alerts him or her to take note.

Be direct. "Sam, let's talk about something else. I think Ms. Enright would be interested in hearing about our company's new test kitchens."

If the rule-breaker is your customer or client and you're reluctant to intervene, try to make an early exit. In the future, arrange to meet this individual in a less public setting. Your grasp of business etiquette dictates you make the other person feel comfortable, but you have every right to feel comfortable, too.

A dining-table setting promotes a small-talk environment, whereas a conference-table setting promotes a let's-get-down-to-business environment. When someone you must do business with is a poor dinner companion, meet him or her at the conference table or somewhere else.

4

Mastering Nonverbal Communication

WHAT SOMEONE'S BODY LANGUAGE SAYS

A policeman arrives at the scene of a crime and two men in the crowd point to you. You let go of the injured victim's wrist and begin to run. The policeman chases you and when he catches up to you, he takes firm hold of your arm.

Pointing, running, using a firm grip—not a word has been spoken, yet a message of accusation, attempted escape, and ultimate capture is broadcast to onlookers. It's a strong message and completely conveyed via an unspoken language.

You remove your wallet from your pocket and show the policeman your identification. He releases your arm and shakes your hand. You smile at one another. He returns to the scene of the crime and you resume your running pace.

Onlookers may not know that you're a doctor who is running up the street to obtain a medical bag from your parked car. They do believe, however, you're no longer a crime suspect.

You may not phrase it in so many words but whether you're at play or at work, you undoubtedly rely upon body language as a vital information source.

- Your boss yawns while you make your presentation to the team.
- Your assistant rises from his chair and places his arms across his chest when you approach his desk.
- You're interviewing for a new position and the interviewer won't make eye contact with you.
- One of your colleagues prefers a chair near the door whenever there's a conference room meeting.

Is your boss bored with your presentation?

Does your assistant feel defiant?

Does the interviewer find you repulsive?

Is a quick get-away your coworker's priority?

What If?

Your boss is tired.

Your assistant is rising to greet you.

The interviewer rarely makes eye contact with anyone.

Your coworker is shy and prefers to exit quickly rather than chat with others when a meeting concludes.

All these interpretations have merit, too.

The office gossip, however, claims your boss has taken a job with another company. Your boss is generally attentive to you and recently gave you an excellent job performance review. Accordingly, you dismiss the notion that your boss is bored or tired and no longer worry that your performance was at fault.

And, so it goes.

Your inquiring mind wants to know what's happening and makes use of all the messages at hand.

WHAT YOUR BODY LANGUAGE SAYS

Someone sends a message. Someone receives it.

If someone is sending you messages via body language, you can be sure that your body language conveys messages, too. It's unsettling to think that your physical movements may tell a keen observer a great deal about you without your knowledge or permission.

If, for example, you find your client is long-winded and you repeatedly allow your eyes to stray from his face to the open window as he drones on, he may conclude you don't have his best interests at heart. No matter how good your product's price is or how satisfactory your promised delivery date, your wandering eyes are likely to make it impossible for you to clinch the sale.

Or suppose you have a deadline to meet and a supplier approaches your desk. You courteously rise to shake his hand but immediately resume sitting. You don't wave him toward a chair as you have done in the past. If he should sit down, you reach for the telephone as you pick up a file from your desk. You're asking him to depart without saying a word.

Subtext Explained

Most people understand body language. Some know it just a little, but others speak it like a native!

If reading the last few paragraphs sums up the time you've spent studying body language, fasten your seatbelt and prepare to navigate to new ground.

Everyday Business Etiquette puts the focus on good manners, top-notch behavior, and a mastery of the rules that helps you to prosper in the business arena. To make the best use of business etiquette, it's essential that you comprehend what Julius Fast refers to as body-language **text and subtext** in his book *Body Language in the Workplace* (NY: Penguin Books, 1991).

Once you master body language, you'll be amazed at how you sharpen all your person-to-person communications and use your know-how to get the results you desire.

> *"The subtext in any exchange is a mixture of many different elements. In part, it is composed of each person's body language, posture, hand movements, eye contact, how he or she handles space, and the ability to use subtle touch at the right moment. The way we use our voices also influences how our words are interpreted. The same sentence can be said in many different ways, ranging from bland disinterest to passionate intensity. Each delivery spells out a different subtext."*
>
> *Body Language In The Workplace*
> (Penguin Books, 1991)

Here, *text* refers to what is said while *subtext* encompasses everything else that's relevant.

Accordingly, body language is composed of: yawns, folded arms, a favored seat near the exit, a drifting gaze, and much more. It's so much more that it easily lends itself to long-term study. Moreover, since you won't find any dictionaries that give you precise meanings, you'll become your own lexicographer.

In their book, *Business in Mexico: Managerial Behavior, Protocol, and Etiquette,* (NY: Haworth, 1994) authors Candace McKinniss and Arthur Natella, Jr., claim that an embrace in a Mexican business setting sends a message of reassurance, not affection. Moreover, while citizens of the United States feel comfortable within eighteen inches to six feet of one another, Mexicans prefer a comfort zone of eighteen to twenty-one inches.

It's immediately obvious that not only must you become a student of body language in the environment in which you grew up, attended school, live, and work but you must be prepared to understand what business people in other lands with whom you'll interact find agreeable or disagreeable.

HOW SMILES, HANDSHAKES, AND NODS CAN HELP OR HINDER

Smile!

Smile when you're being introduced to someone. A smile suggests that you're receptive to meeting this individual as opposed to feeling reluctant. It's a courteous way to approach an individual you're meeting for the first time.

Smile when you're feeling uncomfortable or out of place and you'll mask your concerns. Your confidence level should rise quickly because your smile invites positive feedback from others, which in turn can make you feel better. In business settings, you want to appear to be in charge of yourself and a smile coupled with good posture can work wonders.

Smile when you give or receive a compliment. A smile lends a certain savoir faire to the exchange and helps to punctuate your tribute. When you're the one being praised, you boost your likability quotient when you accept a compliment gracefully. Too many people feel embarrassed or undeserving and if they say something to reveal those feelings, they diminish the other person's position. A smile helps to assure you don't do this.

Smile when you applaud someone. A coworker may deserve an ovation upon public receipt of an honor or after a job well done. On the chance that you're disappointed or expected to be the one who was acknowledged, your smile will help disguise your state of mind. You'll appear to be gracious and a good sport. That's a welcome image to cultivate at work or at play.

Take care not to frown when you don't feel like smiling unless you want to use your body language to show you are offended or dismayed.

A false smile is not a thing of beauty. It generally involves only the lip area of the face and isn't accompanied by smiling eyes or relaxed facial expression. Someone who repeatedly flashes false smiles may soon get the reputation for being a phoney. As mentioned before, a less-than-genuine smile can help you glide into a relaxed or more favorable state of mind but if you frequently sport a false smile, you repel people, the opposite of what you want.

Smiles that last too long invite suspicion. If you're someone's mentor and smile for the full forty minutes this person addresses a group, the audience may understand that you're pleased and proud of this individual. Under most circumstances, however, prolonged smiles make onlookers feel uncomfortable because they suggest the smiler isn't focused on the here-and-now. It's another example of how an extreme action can bring about a reaction that's in opposition to the desired goal.

Handshakes

A firm handshake when you meet or greet a business associate you haven't seen for some time is conventional. Although men and women have shared the business arena for many years, some men are reluctant to extend their hands to a woman unless she first extends her hand. Unless you're rebuffed by a particular individual who indicates she doesn't wish to shake your hand, disregard this once-proper etiquette guideline and extend your hand to greet a business associate, client, supplier, and others without regard to gender.

It's courteous to rise from your chair when you shake someone's hand unless, of course, you're unable to do so due to physical limitations.

Avoid quick, fluttery handshakes that indicate that you're unsure of yourself. Hold the other person's full hand long enough to shake it once or twice. If you grasp at fingertips or extend only a small portion of your hand, the entire greeting is clumsy. You may have to work for several minutes to reach a comfortable rapport which could otherwise have been established quickly with a firm and well-timed handshake.

Lean into a handshake. If you or the other individual pulls away, the greeting ritual is flawed. Although you both smile and share a firm handshake, the act of pulling away suggests something is amiss. If it happens to you more than once, make sure you don't have an unpleasant body odor that prompts others to step back. Powerful perfume odors or tobacco residue on your breath can also be culprits.

Smile or nod your head and look someone in the eye when you shake hands. This behavior rounds out the greeting and takes the stiffness out of the ritual. More importantly, it announces that you're giving the individual your complete attention, which is the courteous thing to do when you greet someone.

Have you ever had someone extend his hand to you while turning his head to speak to someone else? It's a put-down and a turn-off. Don't do it.

Nodding Your Head

Some affirmative head nodding is preferable to a stiff demeanor. An affirmative head nod doesn't necessarily mean that you agree; it may mean only that you understand. A slight head nod is a subtle but positive gesture that also announces you're giving the speaker your undivided attention, and that's a courteous thing to do.

Don't give away your position by shaking your head in disagreement unless you want to deliver this message both to the speaker and to others who are in position to notice.

The speaker may not mind your opposition when it's delivered afterward or when it's delivered privately, but vigorous head shaking when there's a small audience draws attention to you and away from the speaker. This is a rude gesture and not only will you garner the speaker's disfavor, you're likely to be judged as lacking good manners by everyone present. If you hope to win them over to your way of thinking, you don't want to appear to be a coarse individual.

On the other hand, if someone is making what you consider to be an outrageous statement to the group, vigorous head shaking may bring the desired result.

If someone is grimacing at you and shaking his or her head from side to side, take note. You're doing something wrong.

A manager climbed to the podium to announce the arrival of the main speaker and looked off-stage to where his assistant stood shaking her head vigorously from side to side and waving her arms. He ignored her and proceeded. When the speaker stepped on stage to join him, the audience laughed. Instead of a male E. G. Grahan stepping from behind the curtain, they were treated to the arrival of an unmistakably female E. G. Grahan. The manager wouldn't have announced the speaker as Mr. E. G. Grahan if he had heeded his assistant's body language signals.

Too much positive head-nodding can earn you the label, "Yes Man." Take care to use this gesture with some reserve even when your boss or a senior company official repeatedly and sincerely earns your approval.

HOW POSITION-STRATEGIES ACT FOR YOU OR AGAINST YOU

On the first day of class, the student took a seat at the front of the room. By midterm, he opted for a place at the rear of the room. Can you guess why?

His enthusiasm waned.

He became friendly with another student who preferred to sit further back in the classroom and he sat near her.

He didn't want the professor to call upon him so often and thought his front-row seat attracted the professor's attention.

The answers may be all of the above or none of the above. The point is, however, that when you relinquish a favored spot, people tend to notice. They probably speculate on your motives. If you prefer to avoid this kind of scrutiny, choose a different place in the meeting room each time people gather. Don't opt for the same table in the employee cafeteria on every occasion and don't race to the coffee urn as soon as the sweet rolls are delivered.

By not adopting habits of position, you don't provide grist for the rumor mill! If anything, you send a signal that you're a flexible individual who is willing to try new things.

When you rise to your feet and extend your hand for a handshake, you appear to be the more important person if the other person must walk a distance to take your hand. Accordingly, if you make an individual walk a distance to greet you, he or she may resent your "I'm better than you are" body language. Moreover, if the other person is your boss, he or she may think you're being rude.

On the other hand, you may want to play this game if you're scrambling for a leadership position and you want the competition to look as though he or she is in second place.

Sitting next to honored guests or company executives at a company function tends to make you look important, too. If that's your goal, work to obtain a favored chair. If you get it, be prepared to converse intelligently with the individuals seated nearby.

When someone enters your office, if you come around from behind your desk and sit near him or her, you set up a friendly climate for a more relaxed discussion than if you sit behind your desk. The behind-the-desk position is formal, and signifies that this is your turf. Sit in that desk chair if you want to impress a client with your power and know-how. Sit away from the desk when you want to encourage an employee who you believe has asked to see you to impart some sensitive information.

Experts say a tall person commands more respect than a shorter one unless or until he or she spoils the perception. Taller individuals appear to be superior. Whenever possible, use that knowledge to place yourself higher than someone you want to impress. You can, for example, sit at the corner of your desk top and look down upon your visitor who is sitting in a chair. You can stand up when you address coworkers who are seated at a conference table. Position yourself so that others look up to you, literally, and take advantage of this perception. Remember, an opposite position is desirable when you don't want to dominate. In that case, show your visitor to a chair that's on an equal level with yours.

Don't invade someone's personal space. The question is: Where does personal space begin and where does it end? The answer isn't the same for everyone. Personal-space requirements relate, in part, to regional habits. Some people stand practically nose to nose when they confer while others are more than an arm's length away. When in doubt, observe how others who are nearby use space. Don't automatically determine that someone is impolite when he or she stands further away from or closer to you than you're used to.

OPENING AND CLOSING DOORS, AND OTHER TACTFUL MOVES

Holding the Door for Someone

It would be foolish to allow a door to swing back at someone who is following closely at your heels. That's simply a matter of good judgment. There are times, however, when your considerate attempt to hold the door open for someone can make that person uncomfortable. Some younger men bristle if an older woman holds a door open for them.

Do they think she's trying to show them that she's stronger?

Are they being denied the opportunity to display the good manners their parents taught them?

It's sometimes difficult to know why an act of goodwill on your part can be held against you. One-size answers don't fit all.

Generally speaking, hold the door for anyone who may be behind you and about to pass through the door, too. Be alert to responses and avoid repeating actions that make others unhappy. That, after all, is the essence of business etiquette.

When it comes to approaching a door with a small group of people, anyone in the group can hold the door for the others. Many businessmen prefer to open a door for a woman. She should accept the gesture with grace. If she's not thriving in the business arena, holding a door open for her male coworkers won't improve her position.

Open or Closed?

A closed door helps to establish privacy and shields against outside disturbances. If you're visiting a client and he prefers to keep the door open, he may be signaling you that you're not on the inside track.

A closed door at a hotel-room meeting is a different matter. Obviously, the door would be closed. Accordingly, it may not be prudent to arrange a closed-door meeting in an environment where the privacy or intimacy it affords puts anyone at a disadvantage.

A hotel-room meeting between a man and woman, for example, can be fraught with misunderstanding. If you find such a meeting is necessary, arrange for a third party to be present. The hotel concierge may be able to arrange for a secretary to join you. You may want to adjourn the meeting to a more public area in the hotel like the lounge or restaurant.

If you want everyone to know you're approachable, keep your office door open. When you face the pressure of an immediate deadline or are otherwise involved, close the door. If you're scrupulous about when you open or close your office door, your message will be consistent and most people should respect your wishes. It won't be necessary to make excuses and turn people away. Your good image and facility with business etiquette won't be put to the test because the door says it all.

Other Tactful Moves

Be alert for situations in which you can act to put others at ease.

If, for example, your customer is a late arrival at a new equipment training seminar and doesn't have the information packet you distributed at the start of the program, continue your presentation while you stroll to his side and deliver a packet to him. Open it to the correct page and he won't miss a beat. If you do nothing, he'll sit empty-handed until there's a recess, feeling awkward. Your deft moves put him at ease. He'll be grateful.

Or when your client arrives at a dinner meeting with her spouse and no other spouses are in attendance, motion the server to seat the couple near you. By inviting the couple to join you, you indicate they are both welcome. Your smooth acceptance will signal others to make the spouse welcome, too.

Your boss shows up at a stockholders meeting in shirt sleeves while all the other attendees are wearing jackets and ties. You slip off your jacket and hang it on the back of your chair. Two colleagues notice and remove their jackets, too. Your actions take the spotlight off the one individual who perhaps should have thought to dress more formally. Your creative and immediate response effectively neutralized what could have been an embarrassment to your boss and an irritant to stockholders.

THE IMPORTANCE OF LISTENING!

Why, you ask, does the topic of listening fall into the category of mastering nonverbal communication?

You can't listen carefully and speak at the same time. Fine-tuning the courteous art of listening demands that you also curb body language that would interrupt the speaker.

Here are nonverbal messages that may distract or discourage a speaker: a facial grimace, moving back or away from the speaker, fidgeting in your chair, gazing around the room or frequently looking away from the speaker, gazing fixedly into the distance, shuffling papers, waving to someone who enters the room.

Can you think of other body-language statements that would discourage someone who is trying to impart information to you and expects to have your undivided attention?

How about one knee crossed over the other and your foot bouncing up and down, or a bemused expression on your face?

What Does It Mean?

If you want to be viewed as a good listener, develop the demeanor a winning poker player carefully cultivates. When your boss, a client, a coworker, or a friend or family member speaks to you, take the time to listen to the individual and listen well. Listen as though you were a blank slate waiting for the speaker's chalk. Aside from all the other benefits you stand to gain, you'll enhance your professional image. The speaker will think of you as bright (after all, your undivided attention shows that the speaker is important, and he or she is sure to agree with you), dependable, sympathetic, and understanding.—You get the idea.

Author Terry Ward lists listening, along with writing and speaking, as one of the twelve secrets of business success in her book, *Smart Women at Work: 12 Steps to Career Breakthrough* (Chicago: Contemporary Books, 1987).

In Michael Thomsett's *The Little Black Book of Business Etiquette* (NY: American Management Association, 1991), Thomsett discusses the challenge of critical listening when you're engaged in a telephone conversation. He admonishes readers to listen carefully to how they perform on the telephone when they can't rely upon their nonverbal language to help them convey a message. Thomsett recommends that you listen carefully for the mistakes others make when they speak to you over the telephone.

How can someone who is invisible be discourteous? He or she might ask you to hold the line and leave you waiting—repeatedly. Or you may hear the sound of desk drawers opening and closing or papers being shuffled on a desk, a drink being sipped or gum being chewed, or the sound of someone talking in the background, probably someone who has been invited into the room by the person you believe is listening to you.

In short, whether body language is visible, as in a face-to-face confrontation, or invisible, as during a telephone conversation, it's essential that you exercise the same good manners and make every effort to give the speaker your undivided attention. That's the first step in being a good listener.

There's more:

1. *Don't think about what to say to the speaker until you've heard everything he or she has to say. If you do, you're distracted and don't absorb all that is said. Moreover, your response may be different once you hear all the details.*
2. *If you find your attention waning, focus your eyes on the speaker's face or, if on the telephone, cast your glance upward to a ceiling or some other blank space so that you can concentrate on what you're hearing.*
3. *If the room or environment is noisy, interrupt the speaker and ask that you both retire to a quieter place so that you can hear everything he or she has to say.*
4. *If feasible, delay the conversation if you feel agitated or pressured by other tasks. Set an appointment to get together at a time when you'll be able to listen carefully. Although the individual may be disappointed about having to wait, he or she should respect your desire to secure a special time and place to focus on what's important to him or her.*

Listen Carefully to Everyone

Consider everyone with whom you communicate as you work:

- a spouse or significant other
- your child's caretaker or teacher
- boss
- clients
- coworkers
- vendors
- transportation suppliers or garage attendants
- telephone operators
- secretaries and support staff

- staff at a favored eatery
- your dry cleaner
- your hair stylist

You communicate with these individuals on a steady basis and as a result, you must listen to them. When you're courteous and listen carefully, you obtain valuable information and you may be able to favorably influence their behavior.

When you satisfy most of the players in your business circle you automatically take career steps forward. When they're all in your corner, there's no telling how many giant steps forward this group contributes to your success.

5
Courteous Behavior with Members of the Opposite Sex

APPLY THE RULES OF BUSINESS ETIQUETTE TO AVOID MISUNDERSTANDINGS

Sexual harassment is a crime.

In order to distinguish between men's and women's behavior toward one another in the workplace that may be inappropriate but not a criminal act, it's important to define sexual harassment.

What is Sexual Harassment in the Workplace?

- Unwelcome or unwanted sexual advances
- Requests or demands for sexual favors, and
- Other verbal or physical conduct based on gender when this behavior:
  —Is a term or condition of employment (explicit or implicit)
  —Is used as a basis for employment decisions
  —Unreasonably interferes with work performance or creates an intimidating, hostile or offensive working environment

This definition is contained in 1994 training materials issued by the Equal Employment Opportunity Office of Tucson, Arizona, entitled, *Sexual Harassment in the Workplace.*

The law firm of Snell & Wilmer with offices in Phoenix and Tucson, Arizona; Orange County, California; and Salt Lake City, Utah published a booklet, *Sexual Harassment* (1994), which they make available, as a community service, to employers.

Authors William R. Hayden and William P. Allen write,

> "Sexual Harassment is a form of gender discrimination prohibited by various federal, state and local civil rights laws. The courts and the Equal Employment Opportunity Commission generally define sexual harassment as unwelcome conduct of a sexual nature that affects or interferes with an employee's work environment."

Hayden and Allen also write, "Because sexual harassment is situational and closely dependent upon perception, intent and context, it is impossible to formulate a list of rules of conduct that would preclude exposure to claims of sexual harassment."

Accordingly, it's not possible for *Everyday Business Etiquette* to provide a blueprint for action which will safeguard readers against serious accusations or confirm that specific actions constitute a crime. Moreover, *Everyday Business Etiquette* is not and should not be considered a source for legal advice. Specific questions and concerns regarding sexual harassment should be discussed with an attorney or qualified experts.

To contact the nearest Equal Employment Opportunity Commission (EEOC) office, telephone (800) 669-4000. You will be directed to the appropriate office. For information regarding EEOC procedures and regulations, call (800) 669-EEOC. Information is available in both English and Spanish.

It is possible to examine everyday occurrences and offer valuable do's and don'ts for interaction between the sexes. You'll find that these do's and don'ts are largely common-sense methods that will help you to better shape your own performance.

Although the majority of sexual harassment claims are filed on behalf of women, men can and do file claims against women and same-sex harassment claims are not unknown. In a federal court in Wyoming, male employees took action against their male supervisor based upon offensive sexual remarks directed at them concerning their wives.

In recent years, sexual harassment has been in the spotlight on radio and television talk shows, in newspaper and magazine articles, and as the subject of books and movies.

"Can Men And Women Work Together?" is the title of an article that appeared in *Parade Magazine* (March 20, 1994). In it, writers Dianne Hales and Dr. Robert Hales report that the number of sexual harassment cases soared after Anita Hill's testimony at the confirmation hearings for Supreme

Court Justice Clarence Thomas in 1991, during which Ms. Hill accused Justice Thomas of sexual harassment. The article outlines "10 Golden Rules" for men and women to use in what's referred to as "these better-safe-than-sorry times."

Be aware that sexual harassment isn't necessarily about sex, either. Experts say it's about power. Its goal is domination and humiliation and has nothing to do with caring or with love. If men and women are to work together without fear of becoming either "the accused" or "the victim" it's important to agree that today's ideal workplace is one in which men and women can't settle for anything less than mutual respect.

How Courtesy Makes a Difference

Business etiquette is practiced to make people comfortable with one another so that business can prosper.

The following guidelines suggest how to act in a business-like manner to achieve goals and avoid misunderstandings:

Limit physical contact to a handshake rather than a hug or a pat

Even when you know a person very well, a business setting is not the environment for lingering embraces or other tactile displays of affection. Kind words will often suffice and nothing more is necessary.

When you want to be complimentary, focus on business skills, not on someone's physical appearance

A woman might like the way a colleague looks in his blue suit when he addresses visiting dignitaries. She's on safer ground when she limits her compliment to the enthusiastic way his audience responded to his comments.

Men should avoid comments regarding a woman's beautiful hair, pretty dress, or other physical attributes. A woman may be able to compliment another woman about those things but a male coworker should stick to complimenting the woman's business know-how and achievements.

Some employee relations consultants favor using the same standards for members of either sex. They advise complimenting on merit, **never** on physical appearance. If you think it's preferable to maintain the same standard for all, by all means do so.

What happens if a coworker sheds sixty pounds and you know she worked hard to attain this result? Can you say something about her appearance?

How can you not?

She'll probably be pleased to hear that you applaud her self-discipline and perseverance. You might say something generic such as, "You look terrific." That will let her know you've noticed the effort she's made.

Criticize harassing behavior but don't criticize a person

It's a successful management dictum to criticize an employee's action or deed rather than the employee. It tends to get results while eliminating the need for face-saving posturing. Some examples are as follows:

- "Sam, terms of endearment can be demeaning in the office. When a secretary is called dear or honey customers and coworkers within earshot won't view her as a capable assistant. They'll be reluctant to confer with her and she'll be less effective in her job through no fault of her own. In addition, I'm sure Ann prefers to be called by her given name."
- "Off-color jokes can offend. Even though some customers laugh when you tell your dumb-blond jokes, a few customers squirm. It's not worth losing even one customer's goodwill over a joke."

Don't send a gift to a business associate's home unless you do it as part of a group.

One young manager inspired the ire of an executive's wife when she mailed a small gift for the executive to their home. She thought she would advance her standing in the company with a gift congratulating the executive for winning a major account for the firm.

In general, business gifts should be exchanged on business turf. Moreover, they should be tasteful and not hint at a romantic interest. Intimate apparel is obviously a no-no, but avoid flowers and candy, too. Simply because they're a convenient selection, you might send them to a business acquaintance, but think twice before doing so. This is especially true when you're the only one presenting the gift. Group gifts, by their very nature, don't carry a suggestion of romantic intentions.

If you're offended, say so

When you're offended by an off-color or suggestive comment, say so. It's courteous to avoid saying anything when you can't say something pleasant in most business exchanges, but this is an exception. Try to comment on the deed rather than the person. End with a question that summons the offensive individual to react.

Action and reaction can promote change. If you don't react, this person has no reason to change. If you make this person react, something positive may result.

"Hank, stop undressing every pretty girl who passes with your eyes! It's embarrassing!" may be quick and to the point but it's more professional to say, "Hank, ogling members of the opposite sex is a trait you wouldn't expect from a mature professional in a business setting. Don't you agree?"

Avoid lonely after-hours office meetings

When the staff has left for the day and a male and female employee frequently stay later to work, they're bound to start tongues wagging. Use good judgment when you arrange business meetings that include yourself and only one member of the opposite sex. If you must work late at the office, ask a third person to stay for the late work, too. And, if you're asked to join a colleague alone in a remote setting, request a change of venue. Consider appearances. It's distressing to have to deny rumors that are truly unfounded. Don't provide grist for the mill!

GENDER SENSITIVE DON'TS

Very often an offender is surprised to learn that his jokes or shenanigans offend anyone. When confronted, he might think the one who is complaining isn't serious or may even go so far as to suggest she or he should lighten up. After all, friends and family aren't offended. They laugh with him and know it's all in fun.

A male supervisor joked that a female employee was wearing a padded bra, said she looked nice, and asked if she was "going hooking." He told a male coworker in her presence that "if you guys have anything going on, let me be the first to know," and he said he wanted her body.

Funny?

Not in court, where it was found that the female employee was subjected to a "hostile work environment." (*Guiden v. Southeastern Public Service Authority of Virginia*, 1991).

Pictures of women in the nude and in various stages of undress appeared throughout the workplace in magazines, clippings, calendars, and plaques on the walls at a shipyard. The court concluded that the conduct constituted an extensive and pervasive "visual assault on the sensibilities of female workers."

(*Robinson v. Jacksonville Shipyards, Inc.*, 1991).

Do these actual case citations surprise you?

Would you choose to ignore this behavior?

Can taking action benefit everyone involved?

Dr. Kenneth L. Lloyd, author of *Sexual Harassment, How to Keep Your Company Out of Court* (Panel Publishers, NY, 1992), claims most victims' first response is to ignore harassment and later to deny it. The individual can't believe it's happening to her or him.

When you act early, alone or with coworker support, you may be able to stop obnoxious behavior before it escalates.

Kenneth Lloyd's Special Report for executives tells them how to prepare company policies and enforce them. When top management is serious about maintaining an atmosphere that nurtures mutual respect, harassment practices are dealt a serious blow!

You're acting properly when you take advantage of the system your company has in place to challenge obnoxious and offensive behavior.

Lloyd lists formal training as one of the steps in a sexual-harassment prevention program.

If you're in a management position or if you feel that your work environment needs improvement to promote mutual respect, you may want to recommend training programs for all employees.

Sensitivity-training films and discussions led by individuals who specialize in sexual harassment prevention can help everyone to enjoy a workplace that supports each person's dignity and freedom to do his or her job.

COURTEOUS RESPONSES TO TACTLESS BEHAVIOR

Rude, thoughtless, inconsiderate—it's all the same and it's the kind of behavior that makes people feel angry.

It's important that you compose yourself before responding, so that you control what you say. When you're angry, it's easier to say something you may regret.

Something tactless, perhaps?

Moreover, you must decide whether it's best to let the comment or omission pass. On occasion it's best to do nothing.

Review the following courteous responses to tactless behavior and feel free to adapt them to your needs:

A colleague says: "She's asking for it when she wears a tight skirt. I'll bet she loves it, too. Trashy dames like her deserve what they get."

Response: "Bill, don't tell me you buy into that old myth that women who dress suggestively deserve to be harassed. Nonsense. Doesn't your sister, (wife or daughter) wear those newer tight skirts, too? It's part of today's fashion."

A supplier says to a secretary, "Your boss is working because she wants to find herself a husband."

Response: "Is your boss only working to find himself a wife? All this time I thought they were working to make a living."

A woman refuses a lunch invitation. The executive who was refused comments to a colleague, "That one plays hard to get."

Response: "No is no, Jack. If I were you, I wouldn't ask her again. Maybe she'll invite you sometime. If not, forget it."

A male office manager frequently approaches women employees from behind and massages their necks and shoulders. He's often asked to stop, but doesn't.

Send him a thank-you note with the invoice from a local exercise and spa establishment. Make sure the women he annoys with his massages sign the note. Add a line or two: "We know how you value massage, so we engaged the services of professionals at the ABC Spa. Since you're such a proponent of massage, we knew you'd want us to send you the bill. Thanks."

Try honesty, try poking fun, try taking someone by surprise. As the foregoing examples illustrate, it's possible to be well mannered while you sock it to them!

> *"Opinion is ultimately determined by the feelings, and not by the intellect."*
>
> Herbert Spencer (*Social Statics,* 1851)

In other words, appeal to someone's feelings (e.g., shame, foolishness), not just the intellect, and he or she should retreat from unacceptable behavior.

Think how sweet your success will be when you're the catalyst for positive change but haven't compromised your own well-mannered style!

HOW TO BEST SIZE UP YOUR AUDIENCE

Some members of an audience are attentive. Some aren't.

When a male coworker repeatedly says, "I'm sorry," but never changes his ways he's inattentive. He may not believe requests are bona fide, or he may not understand the meaning of a promise.

Bottom line?

Your performance may have to be noisy and a little outrageous if you're going to get his attention.

On the other hand, when another colleague uses inflammatory gender-descriptive slang once or twice, you may decide to let it pass because his deportment is usually exemplary.

Once you size up your audience you may:

- Let offensive behavior pass without comment.
- Confront an individual personally.
- Ask another coworker to join in the confrontation.
- Ask an intermediary to confront the individual.
- Enlist the aid of your boss or a senior executive.
- Look outside your company for guidance from experts on sexual harassment.

FOUR CASE HISTORIES OF SEXUAL HARASSMENT COMPLAINTS

For purposes of this exercise, actual cases have been reviewed and adapted. Citations are not included, nor are detailed explanations, since the interest being served is informative and not legal.

Case Number One

An employee was dismissed shortly after she refused her boss's request for a date. She had a poor attendance record and other employees with equally poor attendance records had been dismissed. Nevertheless, she maintained she was a victim of sexual harassment because she wasn't dismissed until after she refused the boss's request for a date.

Your judgment? Please choose one:

1. *A request for a date doesn't imply a request for sexual favors. Her dismissal wasn't the result of refusing the invitation from her boss. Her poor record of attendance was a valid reason for job loss.*
2. *Since the dismissal followed almost immediately after the employee refused the date, she probably was dismissed because she refused her boss.*

The expert decision:

The court determined the employee didn't show she wouldn't have been fired based on her poor attendance record. She didn't or couldn't demonstrate refusal to date her boss was reason for dismissal. The employee lost her case.

If you had a poor record of attendance and knew that the loss of your job was imminent, would you feel pressured if your boss asked for a date? If so, how would you respond? The best answer has two parts.

Everyday Business Etiquette logic dictates that you can't ignore a poor attendance record. You should address the problem with management.

- Discuss the reasons for your poor attendance record with your employer.
- Do so as soon as possible since you know the company dismisses employees for this infraction.
- Indicate you have a plan to remedy the situation and offer a specific time when your attendance will improve. If, for example, you have a child-care problem that will be alleviated in six weeks when a relative is free to care for your child, let your employer know about this plan.
- Indicate that you're willing to work to make up for lost time once the child-care problem is solved.

When you're courteous, you consider other people's needs even when you have your own concerns. If management doesn't tolerate chronic absenteeism, it's because absenteeism negatively impacts the company's ability to serve customers.

Everyday Business Etiquette logic dictates that you can say "no" without offending anyone. This is true even when you don't find the offer appealing and want the individual to be discouraged from making another offer.

- "Thanks, but I'm not dating. My husband and I are separated but we're attempting a reconciliation. You were kind to ask me."
- I guess I never mention it at the office, but I've got a special girl in my life. I feel pleased to be asked but I've got to decline. Thank you."
- "I feel honored by your invitation but I must decline. Thank you."

Extending a personal invitation to someone can be risky business. You must expose your feelings. A refusal makes you feel vulnerable as well as disappointed. A considerate person recognizes this truth and takes care to say "no" as politely as possible.

Everyday Business Etiquette practices will result in a better outcome than that described in Case Number One.

Case Number Two

A state trooper resigned her position and cited coworkers' horseplay as her reason for leaving. She claimed she had been compelled to resign and therefore should be considered discharged and entitled to appropriate benefits and considerations.

Your judgment? Please choose one:

1. *Horseplay may be annoying but it probably isn't a crime (i.e., sexual harassment). If she was disturbed by this behavior she could have made an effort to influence change. Resigning was a drastic step and she has to live with the consequences.*
2. *A state trooper's job can be dangerous. If she believes her coworkers' behavior is offensive, she may feel they won't act in a responsible manner when called upon to act in the line of duty. She's right to resign and want the record to show she had no choice.*

The expert decision:

The horseplay of the trooper's coworkers did not rise to the level of sexual harassment. A court determined that a reasonable person would not have felt compelled to resign. Her claims of constructive discharge were not upheld.

If you are troubled by horseplay you find to be offensive and if you work in law enforcement, at a hospital, or in some capacity where snap decisions and mature judgment can have life-and-death consequences, how would you respond to culpable coworkers?

Everyday Business Etiquette logic suggests that you get a second opinion. Horseplay that approaches silliness may be one way coworkers let off steam and keep in shape to perform their demanding jobs. Judging others is a delicate matter and unless you can be objective you may arrive at a questionable conclusion.

Consideration for others and for what makes them tick is essential if you aim to do the right thing.

- If you continue to find the horseplay offensive and problematic, enlist the aid of management to address the problem.
- If you come to believe you can't perform well with this group of people, weigh your options. Can you transfer to another department? Can you

work a different shift? Can you work hard and get promoted away from the situation?

Weighing options and making better choices are often at the crux of techniques that bolster good business results.

What are my options?

Should I or shouldn't I?

Although the following quote comes from a book on the political process, the words apply to critical thinking and planning when it comes to success in the business arena, too.

> *We must dare to think "unthinkable" thoughts. We must learn to explore all the options and possibilities that confront us in a complex and rapidly changing world. We must learn to welcome and not to fear the voices of dissent. We must dare to think about "unthinkable things" because when things become unthinkable, thinking stops and action becomes mindless.*
>
> James William Fulbright (*The Arrogance of Power*)

Case Number Three

A supervisor was dismissed after several female employees complained that he repeatedly asked them out for drinks in spite of their repeated refusals, touched them in offensive ways, and threatened newly hired female employees that they wouldn't become permanent employees if they didn't "please him" during the customary probation period, the first ninety days of employment.

He claimed they misunderstood his attempts to be friendly and the company had no right to fire him. He wanted his job back.

Your judgment? Please choose one:

1. *When the same accusations are made by several employees there's little room for doubt that this supervisor is guilty of sexual harassment. Management acted appropriately when they fired him.*

2. *Management should have enrolled this supervisor in a sensitivity training course. Dismissal was too drastic an action to take.*

The expert decision:

The court upheld the company's termination of this supervisor who was found to have sexually harassed subordinate female employees.

If people are obnoxious and don't treat you with respect, your best choice is to distance yourself from them. Act fast to make changes!

Case Number Four

A truck driver complained to the terminal manager that her codriver sexually harassed her. She asked to be reassigned to another run and another driver. The terminal manager said he asked the codriver if he had harassed the female truck driver and was told, "no." The manager told the female truck driver that he wasn't going to change her assignment. She quit. She felt wronged and took legal action.

Your judgment? Please choose one:

1. *The terminal manager shouldn't believe the female truck driver and not believe the male driver. If assigning her to another run and another driver wasn't convenient, why should he do so? He acted correctly.*
2. *The female truck driver made a serious charge against the other driver. Even though it was her word against his, the terminal manager shouldn't have refused her what could have been a simple remedy.*

The expert decision:

The court stated that an employer doesn't always have to believe an allegation of sexual harassment or to take corrective action. But, was it reasonable to force the female truck driver to choose between going out on the road again with this man or quit her job? The court said no.

The court wasn't convinced that the terminal manager and company fulfilled their obligations to the female employee. She won her case.

If you were faced with a your-word-against-his complaint and found you couldn't have an immediate remedy, what would you do?

Everyday Business Etiquette logic suggests there may be an intermediary step between an immediate remedy and making an exit.

You could refuse to work with this individual while an investigation is pending. Even though you know you're right, it's important to recognize that your supervisor doesn't have sufficient information to make a decision.

The other person may honestly feel wronged if he didn't intend to overstep the boundaries of what constitutes appropriate behavior with a member of the opposite sex. If he knows he's wrong, he may not confess.

His objection or his silence puts the manager in a difficult position.

The manager may offer to add a third employee to your team, so you don't have to be alone with the harasser. This may be an agreeable compromise for all concerned.

Compromise is achieved through the tactful application of give-and-take. Tact is an essential business etiquette component.

THE PITFALLS OF DATING A COWORKER, CLIENT, CUSTOMER, OR SUPPLIER

Many people meet their future spouses at work. Still, an office romance can be hazardous for both a woman and a man. And, dating a major client or a supplier can be troublesome, too.

What happens if the romance sours?

What happens if one person wants to end it and the other doesn't?

What happens when management is aware of the liaison and believes it interferes with job performance?

What happens if the involved individuals are both being groomed for the same executive spot?

What happens when other employees believe an individual gets special preference due to a romantic alliance with a supervisor?

The Answer, Please

The answer to every one of these questions is: your effectiveness at work is in jeopardy.

When you're serious about your career, this is no small matter.

Still, romantic attraction isn't something that obeys a set of rules. It's usually something that just happens.

Discretion

The person who attracts you may be the one you're about to go into the happily-forever-after with and that's no small matter, either.

Proceed with caution. Do your best to keep two sides to your relationship, the office side and the away-from-the-office side. Should the initial flurry of excitement fade and the relationship fail, neither of you will have put your jobs at risk or your professional judgment into question.

Be aware that company policy may frown on a supervisor dating a subordinate employee. Such a situation can be fraught with problems, not the least of which are nepotism policies at some companies that may eventually force one of you to leave the company's employ.

> *"Discretion is the better part of virtue,*
> *Commitments the voters don't know about can't hurt you."*
>
> Ogden Nash (*The Old Dog Barks Backwards,* 1972)

Substitute the word coworkers for the word voters and it's useful advice for an office romance.

If you learn that someone at the office is dating a coworker, and the couple is attempting to be discreet about it, your courteous response must be one of discretion, also. Don't let anyone know that you know.

Silence is golden! Mum is the word! Loose lips sink ships!

In addition to being considerate and showing respect for others' right to privacy, your discretion protects you. If you hint at what you know about coworkers who are dating, you may be confronted by a manager who asks you prying questions about the couple. What will you reply? Or suppose a romantically involved coworker asks you for a favor that will advance the romance:

"Could you change your vacation time with Mary? I can't ask Carla or John because they wouldn't understand. Mary and I want to go away together."

If you're discreet about what you know, you'll be free to be an observer and not a player.

Owing to the precarious nature of office romances, you're probably in the favored position!

6

At-the-Podium Protocol

COURTEOUS MUST-KNOW METHODS A SUCCESSFUL SPEAKER EMPLOYS

Everyone who speaks to an audience knows that it's important to have something to say! Given that,

- How do you look?
- How do you sound?
- Is the room temperature comfortable?
- Is the lighting okay? Not too bright or too dim?
- Are audience chairs comfortable and well arranged?
- Would a chair-and-table arrangement be better than chairs only?
- If paper and pen or other literature is to be made available to the audience, is it in place?
- Can everyone see you and hear you?
- Is your slide program in good condition? How about other visual aids? Are they clean and sharp and able to be viewed by everyone?
- Will you end your remarks before people begin to fidget from boredom or exhaustion?

Not only will your podium experience be more successful if you scrutinize details, your well-looked-after audience will be ready and able to benefit from your presentation. Distractions will be eliminated and conditions will be optimum.

Dotting the i's

A professional speaker who presents seminars all over the country earns a big fee for a day's work and also a percentage of the sales of books and audio material sold to seminar attendees. These materials are related to her topic and she pitches some of them to her audience as truly valuable aids.

After she'd been at her job for about six months, she noticed that her income from materials sold was highly erratic.

She reviewed all the components that come into play at a seminar. She learned that when all the elements were virtually the same (i.e., similar number of attendees and prices for available products, a competent assistant on-site to assist buyers with their selections), the seminars that were held at well-appointed conference centers provided her with the greatest dollar income.

She was convinced the lack of distractions was a key to her success. Too hot, too cold, too thirsty, hard chairs—all this and more caused attendees to lose their focus. Attendees who were well focused maintained their enthusiasm and this probably contributed to better sales figures.

After that analysis, she was especially attentive to all the little details before she stepped to the podium. She realized her study of her six-month experience was hardly conclusive, but she was convinced she achieved more when her audience achieved more.

This is probably true for all speakers. Even if you aren't selling anything more than your opinion, to do everything possible to make your audience comfortable you will:

- Arrive early.
- Ask yourself what would make you happy if you were an attendee and then do everything within your power to grant those wishes.

BETTER AND BEST WAYS TO INTRODUCE THE SPEAKER

There are good, better, and best methods to employ for any challenge you must tackle. Don't settle for a good way to introduce a speaker. Concentrate on finding the best way to do the job. If you begin with this mindset, your comments will energize the audience and delight the speaker.

- Tell the audience something about the speaker that relates to the speaker's topic.
- You'll be able to use words of praise that modesty won't permit the speaker to use about himself or herself. Take advantage of this unique

position and give the audience pertinent background information they're not likely to hear elsewhere. For example, for a business audience gathered to hear about continuing education, the following introductions are appropriate:

—"Our speaker, Marge Beck, was graduated from high school when she was fourteen years old, graduated from college at age seventeen, and earned the first of three post-graduate degrees at the age of twenty.

"As owner and operator of BCA Warehouse Supplies, Inc. she instituted a program to encourage employees to earn college degrees. Today, thirty-four men and women are employed at Ms. Beck's company and twenty-nine of them are college graduates. All twenty-nine college graduates received tuition reimbursement assistance from Ms. Beck's company. She's an employer who backs up her words with deeds. Please welcome Marge Beck."

—"William Trubeck's relaxed manner and quick smile can be disarming. This soft-spoken gentleman will set you completely at ease.

"It's difficult to believe that this modest and unassuming man is a consultant to monarchies the world over and frequently visits Washington to advise the President's advisors.

"Ladies and gentlemen, you're with the man the phrase in-the-know was designed for when you're with William Trubeck, Personal Image and Corporate Image Advisor. It's both an honor and a pleasure for me to introduce Mr. William Trubeck."

- In addition to obtaining the speaker's biography, ask if there's anything the speaker wants the audience to know: "If you were introducing yourself, what would you tell the audience?"

- Even when you have plenty of time, keep the introduction brief and to the point.

- Don't try to be humorous unless it comes easily to you. It's your job to prepare the audience for the speaker and the speaker for the audience. If your attempts at levity go over like a lead balloon, you can't attain your goal.

- Check facts. If you're working from a dated sheet of information, it may no longer be accurate. Make certain you know how to pronounce names. If necessary, contact the speaker's office and confirm the pronunciation with a secretary. Make phonetic notes for yourself (e.g., Major sounds like May-Hor).

If you're rising to introduce one or two speakers, you probably won't need much time to get ready. If, however, you're acting as master or mistress of ceremonies for a longer program, it may be necessary to prepare a few words of thanks when each speaker departs and before the next speaker is introduced.

Take note of how large the stage is, how far people must walk to reach the podium, and where you'll be stationed. You'll want to establish a comfortable rhythm so there's not a lot of "dead air" when people move about on stage, and so that one or two speakers are thanked while one or two are not.

WHAT YOU SHOULD KNOW ABOUT FLAGS, ANTHEMS, AND SEATING ARRANGEMENTS

When you follow the rules for correct placement of flags, you take steps necessary to show respect for your country, state, and company, and for the flags of other countries when they're displayed, too.

This is not a responsibility to be taken lightly. A blunder offends members in the audience who are better informed regarding protocol and who may look upon your breach of etiquette as an attack on patriotism, or your lack of information as unforgivable!

Flag Placement

According to *The World Almanac and Book of Facts 1996* (Funk and Wagnalls, Mahwah, NJ, 1995) a uniform code of etiquette for the flag of the United States was adopted by a joint resolution of Congress, June 22, 1942.

Refer to the code of etiquette appearing in the Funk and Wagnalls publication for information about flag use and display. Or you may write to The National Flag Foundation (Flag Plaza, Pittsburgh, PA 15219) to obtain detailed information on flag etiquette.

Everyday Business Etiquette offers At-the-Podium Protocol but directs you to these sources for additional information in the event you require it.

According to the code of etiquette, in an auditorium, "the flag may be displayed flat, above, and behind the speaker. When displayed from a staff in a church or public auditorium, the flag should hold the position of superior prominence, in advance of the audience, and in the position of honor at the clergyman's or speaker's right as he faces the audience. Any other flag displayed should be placed on the left of the clergyman or speaker or to the right of the audience. . . . When the flag is displayed horizontally or vertically against a wall, the stars should be uppermost and at the observer's left."

When displaying a group of flags at a meeting or company gathering, the U.S. flag is always positioned on the speaker's right (the audience's left), which is the place of honor. The state's flag or company's flag is positioned on the opposite side, to the left of the speaker.

When the United States flag is displayed with flags representing other countries, it should be to the speaker's right (the place of honor). If it's on a platform with flags from other countries, it should be in the center position and slightly elevated. The other flags should be of the same size, each with a separate pole, and displayed in a straight line.

Experts explain that in times of peace, it's not acceptable to display the flag of one nation above another nation. The flag of the United States, however, should be accorded a place of honor in any business environment within the United States.

National Anthem

When "The Star-Spangled Banner" is sung, everyone rises and remains standing at attention. It's proper to cover one's heart with the right hand. When the anthem of another country is played, everyone rises but only citizens of that country salute.

So when a foreign visitor rises for "The Star-Spangled Banner," he or she demonstrates respect for our country and displays good manners. Don't be dismayed, however, if the visitor doesn't respond with a hand over the heart. This gesture is appropriate for citizens of the country the flag represents.

Special Seating Arrangements

You may oversee a meeting with various titled people seated on stage. Ascertain protocol, beforehand, for assigning seats, so you don't unintentionally insult an elected official, a judge, professor, member of the Armed Services, or some other titled attendee.

If you do insult someone, you are not likely to be the only one who is criticized. The company you represent and your business associates may be subjected to chastisement and ridicule for this inappropriate behavior, too.

It may be necessary to research guests' official ranks. There are numerous offices of protocol you may contact for information, as well as a dignitary's home office:

- The Office of Protocol, Department of State (Ceremonial Section), in Washington, telephone (202) 647-1735

- The United Nations Office of Protocol in New York City, telephone (212) 963-1234

When It's up to You

When you're arranging a podium to include numerous dignitaries of high rank, you'll probably discuss plans with their representatives prior to the important day. Experts who handle these chores for city officials and convention centers say there's not always a set of rules one can turn to for guidance. Many decisions are reached by staff people who discuss among themselves the most reasonable arrangement. They consider these factors:

- Who is the host or hostess?
- What is the goal of the gathering?

A city mayor, for example, may be hosting an event to welcome a large company to town. The company will provide 800 new jobs for local people.

If the company produces military supplies, a representative of the military may be in attendance, along with the mayor, governor, Congress members, and the top management of the firm. Though the mayor doesn't outrank the other elected officials, he may be the one who authorized this gathering and who expects to be showcased. The CEO of the company that is being welcomed may be next in rank to the mayor for the purposes of this function. The other attendees will be seated according to rank, if that pattern is clear-cut.

Through discussions with the attendees' trusted assistants, you can usually arrive at satisfactory seating arrangements and speaking order. When an official has been advised of the work that went into planning the seating arrangements and learns that an assistant took part in the decision-making process, he or she is more likely to be satisfied with the assigned seat.

The most considerate thing you can do is to remove the element of surprise, so all attendees feel welcomed and important even though they can't all sit in the one seat of honor.

You may ask, which seat is that?

It's the seat to the right of the host, according to protocol expert Letitia Baldrige. The second-ranking guest sits at the right of the second-ranking company executive.

Moreover, to be seated on the podium is an honor in itself. All who are being so honored should be reminded that this is so.

MAKING PLANS FOR SPECIAL GUESTS BEFORE AND AFTER THE GATHERING

When a special guest is invited to participate at a company function, you'll want to treat this individual much as you would if he or she was a guest in your own home. If time permits, you may want to invite this person to your home or invite him or her to be your guest for dinner at a restaurant or club before or after the function. Or the CEO may wish to do so, and you'll want to apprise the CEO of this individual's schedule and likely availability.

You can use the following checklist:

(1) *Contact the individual near to the expected time of arrival to confirm plans and notify him or her of last minute changes.* If, for example, a hotel accommodation has been changed, the guest should be notified. Even though this person will be met at the airport and transported to the hotel, the information will permit him to alert a spouse, assistant, colleague or interested party who may need to contact him or her.

If you think this is being finicky, consider the saga of the very tall international motivational speaker who arranged for his Paris tailor to mail his new tuxedo to the Plaza when, in fact, he would be staying at the Ritz.

Not only wasn't the tuxedo located and transported in a timely fashion but the speaker couldn't locate a suitable substitute tuxedo in time for the dinner conference and was greatly distressed at having to wear a business suit while others wore black-tie apparel.

It's not only okay to indulge special guests, it's de rigueur!

(2) *If someone travels for many hours to reach your location, consider what your own needs and desires would be if you were the guest.* A quiet place to rest? A place to stretch your legs? A snack? A beverage? An opportunity to freshen up?

If feasible, offer these opportunities to your guest.

(3) *Some dignitaries travel with a secretary or an escort.* Ask. If the individual isn't traveling alone, you'll want to make the appropriate arrangements for his or her companion. Not only is a last-minute scramble less than chic, it takes you away from other important tasks that must be handled at the last minute.

(4) *If the guest will be presented with flowers*, you may want to put in a discreet call to her secretary to inquire about preferences. If someone sneezes at the mere mention of roses, then you may decide to choose gardenias. If a corsage will be presented, what colors will compliment her dress? Her assistant may be able to share this information with you. Your extra effort can be the frosting on the cake!

(5) *If a guest has special dietary needs,* try to accommodate them with as little fuss as possible. At a dinner conference, for example, a strict vegetarian can't get nourishment from a roast-beef dinner. If you ask the caterer to prepare a special plate for the guest, see that it's presented without fanfare. If the guest's dietary needs are based on religious beliefs or health concerns, a handwritten menu explanation can be placed near the plate. It may announce that no animal fat was used in the preparation of the meal or, that vegetables were steamed, not cooked or flavored with butter or oil.

These special touches don't really take much effort but they can make all the difference in the world to the guest. He or she should be favorably impressed and long remember that your company employs thoughtful and efficient individuals.

(6) *If the guest is staying at a hotel other than one where the function will be held,* consider how the guest will travel to the conference center or appropriate location.

Should you or another company executive stop by the hotel with your car to drive the guest to the function? That's red carpet treatment and illustrates to a guest that he or she is in the company of gracious people!

(7) *Once the function has ended, your Cinderella doesn't turn into a pumpkin.* Be attentive to transportation needs or other wind-down activities. If, for example, the individual is something of a captive in town until late the following day when he or she leaves for the airport, should an invitation be extended for breakfast or for a trip to a local place of interest? If your demonstration of courtesy and consideration has been exemplary up until now, don't drop the ball during these last few hours. Of course, the individual may prefer to entertain himself or herself or may have work to do and be unavailable for anything further. But you will have asked!

DISCUSSING SPEAKERS' FEES AND HONORARIUMS

A speaker's fee is generally determined at the time you engage the speaker. When a business manager handles the speaker's calendar, he or she probably handles this detail and you'll probably be told what the fee is and when it should be delivered before you have an opportunity to inquire. If you learn the speaker's fee is higher than you anticipated, you'll have to determine if it's appropriate to ask for a reduction.

You may be able to make a case for a reduced fee and shouldn't feel uncomfortable about attempting to do so. Remember, you're looking after the interests of your company.

If, for example, all proceeds from an annual company picnic will be donated to a community food bank, say so. If the speaker's fee is reduced, the donation can be more generous. If the speaker's fee is firm, let the matter drop. If necessary, let the speaker's representative know you must obtain approval to disperse this sum. Proceed in a timely fashion so that all parties are clear about the agreement.

If the speaker's fee is expected in advance of the occasion, insist on a written statement of performance.

- Is the fee refunded if the speaker doesn't appear?
- If so, how rapidly is it refunded?
- Will the speaker arrange for someone else to appear in the event he is ill or unable to appear?

The best way to obtain answers is to ask questions. Don't be mesmerized into accepting conditions based on responses that are delivered in a matter-of-fact fashion. It may not be all right with you if a substitute speaker appears. You'll want to make that clear.

The process of engaging a speaker and settling details is much smoother if you dot all the i's and cross all the t's at the outset.

If the speaker is a member of the clergy or local dignitary who doesn't have a set fee for a speaking engagement but expects to receive an honorarium, he or she may tell you in advance what's expected. If not, call the individual's office to learn what's customary.

To some people the subject of money is indelicate when it rewards a personal appearance. Those people will probably arrange for an intermediary to handle the transaction.

If a speaker doesn't expect a monetary reward you may want to present one anyway. Make some quiet inquiry as to what's appropriate so that you don't insult the individual with a sum that's too small. If you've been asked to make a donation to the speaker's favorite charity, take care that the sum is sufficiently generous. An experienced colleague may be able to suggest an appropriate sum. And, if you subscribe to the two-heads-are-better-than-one theory, you'll ask more than one person for feedback.

The Envelope, Please

If you're delivering a check or cash to an individual at the end of the program, have it ready and waiting in a plain envelope. It's relatively easy to be discreet about slipping an envelope to someone. It's wholly inappropriate to count out bills or reach into your pocket to retrieve a wad of cash and meter out payment. You can shake the individual's hand and praise the speech or say thanks while you tender the unobtrusive envelope.

If the speaker is debonair, he or she will place the envelope into a briefcase or pocket without delay. It won't be opened or examined in the presence of others.

LATE SPEAKERS AND NO-SHOWS: WHAT DO YOU DO?

When an audience gathers and the speaker is late, it's poor form to allow the audience to wait without explanation. Don't keep them waiting for more than a few minutes. Consider beforehand how to handle such a situation.

- *Can you change the order of speakers?* The late arrival may be held for last.
- *What will you say if you must step to the podium to explain the delay?* Don't say anything with authority if you don't know it to be true. If, for example, you announce the speaker is delayed and learn soon after that he's not coming, you'll have needlessly placed yourself in an awkward position.
- *If refreshments are available,* arrange for them to be served without delay. Invite meeting attendees to enjoy a soft drink or coffee and relax for a few moments while everyone waits for the speaker to arrive.
- *If the speaker is a no-show, you have two choices: Adjourn or get a replacement.* A senior officer in the company may be well prepared to speak to the audience. Telephone his or her office and explain the dilemma. Don't waste everyone's time if a suitable speaker can't be located. Good manners dictate that you apologize to those assembled and permit them to return to their schedules.

You may decide to send notes of apology. By then, you'll have an explanation for the speaker's absence. Mention the reason in your note. People appreciate being informed. Since time is an honored commodity, it's important to show your regard for wasting someone's time. You don't want to spotlight the disaster, but you do want to let people know that you're disappointed, too.

7

Send a Message with Your Wardrobe Selections

WORKDAY CLOTHING: MORE THAN A COVER-UP

The workplace isn't much different than the theater when it comes to "dressing the part."

A bearded actor with peg leg appears on stage brandishing a sword. He takes large strides and pauses next to a treasure chest overflowing with gold coins. A sweat-stained bandanna is tied around his forehead and he sports an eye patch. His clothing is disheveled. You know nothing about the show in progress but you can tell he's a pirate.

Bingo. You're a winner.

If you're in the pirate business and want people to know it, dress like a pirate. It helps set the stage for the action that follows, you don't waste time saying, "I'm a pirate. I'm fierce." People take one look at you and they know.

If a pirate were to read *Everday Business Etiquette*, he'd know that when he takes his chest full of gold to his local bank, opening a savings account there is likely to be delayed unless he changes his image. Pirates and all others take note: it's much easier to go about your business when you blend into the scene.

Is it the sword that makes the bank transaction difficult? Perhaps it's the eye patch or the bandanna, or could it be both?

Even if a pirate sold his ship and his coins are bounty from a legitimate sale and not ill-gotten gains, he's got a lot of explaining to do.

You may smile at this example, but it demonstrates that business-wardrobe choices are not a laughing matter.

Mastery of business etiquette enables you to make others feel comfortable so the business of business proceeds with greater ease. Your personal appearance contributes to the overall effect.

Send a message with your choices.

- A smooth and finished look suggests you are calm, cool, and collected. It follows that you're capable and probably likable. The following features help to send the message:

  —Well-tailored clothing, a good fit, buttons, zippers, hemlines in good repair. Shoes shined and in good condition.

  —Fabrics that are clean and carefully pressed, and do not wrinkle easily.

  —Colors that flatter your height, weight, personal skin tone, and style. If, for example, you're an accountant, you might stick with dark or muted colors when selecting clothing, though a television personality you respect and admire favors bright colors. You must customize or tailor your choices to your position, not someone else's position.

- An elegant or refined look suggests you have power. It follows that you're confident and efficient.
  These features help to send the message:

  —The features of the finished look, plus—Form-fitting clothing instead of swinging or flowing fabrics, frills, and fussy trimmings.
  —Muted tones and soft colors or classics such as the dark blue suit or the basic black dress.
  —Jewelry that hints at a heritage such as a string of pearls or diamond cuff links. More modern stones and styles should be chosen with great care or not at all.

- A crisp and starchy look suggests you're "all business." It follows that you won't let anyone down and you know how to set and reach goals.
  These features help to send the message:

  —All of the above, with a preference for starched blouses or shirts or those which appear to be starched. Closed top-button shirts or button-down shirt collars, higher-neckline blouses, long sleeves with French cuffs and cuff links.
  —A no-slouch posture so the trouser crease or longer shirt hemline is shown to advantage. Stand up straight and let the fabric covering your lower torso unfurl wrinkle-free. Short skirts need not apply.
  —Jackets that complement an outfit lend an air of formality to your appearance. Choose a length to complement your figure and don't

select a jacket with more than two tones. One color should dominate. No jacket pocket should be without a small handkerchief extending slightly above the edge of the pocket.

- An up-to-the-minute trendy look suggests you're open to new ideas and ready to accept change. It follows that you're eager to contribute, energetic.

These features help to send the message:

—Frequently add trendy clothing items to your wardrobe.
—Adapt colors others tend to shun. Bold colors are preferable. Use them sparingly and you won't appear garish.
—Trendy jewelry and hairstyles add pizzazz.

Your Chosen Image

All of the above help set images that are somewhat subjective, dependent on the eyes of the beholder. Or, as David Hume wrote a long time ago:

Beauty in things exists in the mind which contemplates them.

You may feel differently about what it is that permits you to look the way you wish to look to others, and you must make the final judgment. The recommendations listed above should help to point the way.

If you're not in the habit of reading periodicals or publications that feature articles about fashion, you may want to do so from time to time. If you already enjoy this pastime, look at the material with new eyes. Ask yourself if some of the featured clothing would look good on you. Moreover, would it help you achieve your workplace goals?

Even if you have the budget to accommodate a complete new look, it's prudent to move slowly. Add new garments to your wardrobe with purpose and wait to see how people respond.

- Do associates or coworkers take notice?
- Do you receive compliments?
- Do you feel comfortable in the new garments?

Many years ago a children's shoe manufacturer promised youngsters they could "fly" in the company's play shoe. Some youngsters, no doubt, were ready to take off as soon as their feet were enveloped in the new footwear. You want to be sure you can "fly" in your new garments before you invest dollars in more of the same.

It's Elementary

What else needs scrutiny?

- Hairstyle and hair care, nail care
- Choice of cosmetics, perfumes, after-shave lotions or colognes
- Personal cleanliness, mouthwash, deodorants
- Timely disposal of worn or shabby garments
- Cleaning and pressing of clothing
- Jewelry selection that's appropriate to the work environment
- Handbags, wallets, briefcases, belts, all in good repair

These are the basics that enhance your personal appearance and contribute to the message you send to others. At first, these observations may appear to be so elementary or obvious as to be unworthy of mention. Not so. If you're serious about making positive changes, examine your personal standards in these categories, too, and boost them to new heights.

HOW TO KNOW WHAT TO WEAR

Must you wear a tie? Is a short-sleeved shirt permissible? Can you wear a pair of shorts? Should you wear flat shoes or high-heeled pumps?

Wouldn't it be nice to have a magic wand to wave over your questions and the answer would print out on your personal computer printer?

Here's the easy answer and it's available to you even when there's a power failure.

Have faith in your own judgment

Now that you're a serious student of what's acceptable and appropriate, you know more about what's proper than you may think you know. Make inquiries. Rely upon input from people who may have more or different experiences than you have and people whose judgment you trust. Then make a decision and don't agonize over it (e.g., "Am I over-dressed?" "Should I have worn the navy blue?"). Have faith in your judgment.

When you arrive at your destination go about your business with a self-confident manner. No matter what covers your outer self, your inner self must take charge. A positive self-image enables you to behave with confidence and move ahead to achieve goals. If you conclude that you should have dressed somewhat differently for this occasion, consider it a learning experience. It's quite possible that no one else considered your clothing or personal appearance to be inappropriate. Unless you made an unforgivable gaffe, people were focused on your conduct—which, of course, was beyond reproach!

ACCESSORIES: LITTLE THINGS THAT MAKE A BIG STATEMENT

A sparkly pair of shoulder-length earrings or a tie displaying tactless messages can ruin an otherwise perfect presentation. That's why it's important to choose your wardrobe accessories with care.

On the flip side, accessories can enliven an outfit and add diversity to an otherwise limited wardrobe collection.

One public speaker asked her jeweler to fashion a large gold pin shaped like a spoon for her to affix on her jacket. She pins it opposite her heart and shares her strategy.

"A person reaches for my right hand when we meet and the large gold spoon pin leaps into view. It's rare that someone doesn't ask about the spoon shape. The question is an immediate conversation-opener. I respond that I address people at business gatherings that follow breakfast, lunch, or dinner. I love my work and suspect that's why utensils appeal to me."

She explains that this reply generally invites a smile and sparks a more interesting conversation than one that starts off with comments on the weather, heavy traffic or something equally mundane.

This professional reminds us that accessories can serve unique purposes, too. Rely on your own creative talents to come up with a personal "trademark," if you believe it will support the message you want to send.

Almost anything you wear or carry that decorates or completes your outfit is an accessory. Would the following items help you to execute your "look" more effectively or help you attain another goal?

- Scarves or ties that are distinctly different from those you generally purchase?
- Tie tacks or scarf pins
- Pocket handkerchiefs
- Men's braces (suspenders)

- Vests and sweaters
- Stand-alone jackets (i.e., not suit jackets)
- Hats, gloves
- Jewelry, including wrist watches and watch bands
- Belts
- Handbags, briefcases, wallets
- Socks, stockings
- Button covers
- Women's hair combs and other hair ornaments

Next time you shop for clothing, examine some of the accessories you don't normally consider. You may find that a sales representative can offer useful advice and information. If you think you need a complete evaluation and expert assistance, you may want to engage the services of a personal image consultant. Check the classified section of your telephone book to find an image consultant or see Chapter 14 near the end of *Everyday Business Etiquette* for information on goods and services you may want to know about.

Prepare Yourself

Would it surprise you to learn that Shakespeare wrote these lines for a character in a play: "Bid them wash their faces, And keep their teeth clean" or, that the expression, "Cleanliness is, indeed, next to godliness" comes from a religious sermon?

At the theater, in a house of worship, or any other place, cleanliness is essential. As you prepare yourself and your business wardrobe, pay careful attention to cleanliness.

- Choose an excellent dry cleaner and rotate your clothing into the cleaning process as often as is necessary to keep everything fresh.
- Monitor odors which emanate from products you use. This includes perfumed soaps, colognes, shampoos, after shave lotions and similar products. Some perfectly delightful fragrances "go bad" as they age. Your body chemistry can change, too. Pregnancy, new diet, or a move to a very humid environment can cause your usual hygiene products or fragrances to fail. Know when it's time to retire a bottle of perfume or opt for a more effective deodorant.

- Health problems may give rise to unexpected and offensive body odors. Untreated dental decay, for example, often results in a bad mouth odor. You'll want to correct this condition for your personal well-being. Take care not to offend anyone with dragon breath while you're waiting to be treated.
- Frequent shampoos, regular trips to the barber or hairdresser, timely manicures, and immediate replacement of chipped nail polish all enable you to look tidy.

Cleanliness and careful grooming help you punctuate the positive message you send to others in the workplace. Don't forget these vital basics.

Part Two

Rules of Behavior

8

Invitations

Invitations come in all shapes, sizes and mediums. All invitations should have this in common: they should be tendered with sincerity. If you invite someone to attend a function and you do so only because you think you must, as soon as you make that decision, examine your attitude, summon your enthusiasm, and extend that invitation with sincerity. Once you do, you're bound to follow through in a gracious and courteous manner.

Assume, too, that every invitation you receive is extended with sincerity. Don't waste time wondering, "Did he invite me because he wants me to attend or because he felt obligated?" View any invitation you receive as a genuine request for the pleasure of your company. Once you do, once again, you're bound to follow through in a gracious and courteous manner.

EXTENDING AN INVITATION

Will the invitation be mailed?

If so, will it be printed or penned? Should you contact people by telephone to invite them or simply ask the next time you're face-to-face?

How to decide: If you're extending invitations to a great number of people (more than twelve to fifteen) it's practical to put it in writing. Even when the number of invitations is small, a formal or quasi-formal occasion warrants a written invitation.

If, for example, your company is hosting a breakfast to express thanks for a job well done and a few suppliers are on the guest list, a mailed invitation is in order. If, however, you're inviting several colleagues to be your guests for lunch at a restaurant, you'll probably want to telephone each person with your invitation.

Is the event formal or informal? Do you know the invitees well or not? Are some individuals difficult to reach by telephone? These are some of the questions you'll consider when you determine which form invitations will take.

Written or Printed Invitations?

It may be tempting to communicate electronically and you may routinely use a computer mailbox, telephone answering device, or a facsimile transmission to contact individuals. It's strongly urged you don't use any of these means to extend an invitation. The very nature of efficient electronic communication runs counter to an invitation's intent, which is, to inject some warmth and a personal touch into the request.

Choose the stationery or paper products for your handwritten or printed messages with care. Off-beat colors and patterns, for example, don't complement formal invitations. Paper adorned with tiny flowers or curlicues may be attractive but it's not appropriate for an invitation to major stockholders. Examine the wares a large stationery supplier handles for paper that's appropriate for your needs. You're bound to choose wisely when you consider how the invitation will look to the individual who receives it. Does it set the stage for what's to follow?

When invitations are to be printed for you, don't rely too heavily upon recommended wording you find in the printer's sample book. How often have you received one of these sample-book invitations and found it distinctly different from the originator's style and form?

Your invitation, whether extended on behalf of your company, a professional organization, or yourself, should sound like the party or parties hosting the affair.

How much advance notice should you provide?

You don't always have the luxury of time to extend an invitation eight to ten weeks in advance of the occasion. When you do, however, you make it easier for the people you're inviting to reserve the date on their calendars or rearrange their schedules so they can attend.

How to decide: If a large number of guests is expected to be in attendance and you must provide a head count to a caterer or hotel, ask how much advance notice is needed. Your cooperation supports their efforts to serve you well. In this situation, it's reasonable to extend invitations about ten weeks in advance of the event. You may extend other invitations as little as one week in advance. Always provide advance notice of no more than ten weeks and no less than one week. Unless you're in the habit of dealing with family members or close friends on extremely short notice, it's considerate to follow these guidelines in every realm of your life.

What about response time?

Most people need to examine their calendars before they can reply. So it's not reasonable to expect an immediate response. Others may have to travel great distances to be on location for the event and need time to obtain travel information and consider the feasibility of getting there.

How to decide: If you must confer with the caterer by September 3rd, ask people to respond by August 28. You'll have time to ascertain your total number of attendees and contact anyone who hasn't replied. There's always a chance that an invitation hasn't been delivered so it's permissible to follow up with a telephone call. If the invitation is delivered in person, it's wise to ask for a reply by a particular date in order to avoid confusion.

RESPONDING TO AN INVITATION

It's considerate to reply to any invitation as soon as possible. Of course, you must examine your appointment book to be sure you're free to accept an invitation. It's poor form to say yes and then later back out.

Everyday Business Etiquette strategy dictates that when you accept an invitation, you make every effort to attend the function. It may be tempting to accept another invitation that arrives later, but it's not prudent. It's a small world and you risk offending people who may later learn the truth.

How to Proceed

If the invitation was tendered verbally, you should reply the same way. If it arrived in the mail, use the mail to respond unless you're asked to RSVP by telephone. The rule of thumb is to reply in kind.

A self-addressed stamped envelope is frequently sent along with a reply card for your convenience. Use it. Pen your response. A lengthy explanation of why you can't attend isn't proper. A simple, "Regrets" or "Accept With Thanks" should suffice. Don't forget to include your name! If the invitation asks for "Regrets only" you may only have to mark your calendar and attend the function.

If you're responding to an invitation that's unrelated to business, it's both permissible and friendly to write a note to explain a refusal. Use your personal stationery.

When an invitation is formal, you'll want to use time-honored wording.

When the invitation says: "request the pleasure of your company," the response would be: "accept with pleasure your kind invitation for . . ." Or, "regrets that he is unable to accept the kind invitation of . . ."

Write your response in a pattern of lines that are longer toward the center, shorter at top and bottom.

Here are two samples:

Miss Randy Ray
accepts with pleasure
the kind invitation of
Professional Engineers, LaPaloma Chapter
for Monday afternoon,
September eleventh

Mr. Robert Porter
regrets he is unable to accept
the kind invitation of
Mr. Greg Thorn and Ms. Betty Roth
for Monday, the fourth of May
at half after one o'clock.

9

Gifts

IS A GIFT IN ORDER?

In the business world that's not always an easy question to answer.

Your own company probably has an established policy that tells how you're expected to respond if gifts from suppliers or others with whom the company conducts business are presented. You may not be permitted to accept gifts. Or you may not be able to accept gifts which are considered lavish. Examine this policy, which you'll probably find in your employee handbook, and consider whether or not the individual you wish to present with a gift may labor under similar restrictions.

Don't put someone on the spot by giving a gift he or she isn't free to accept. At the same time, you don't want to appear insensitive by not sending a gift when one is appropriate.

How should you proceed?

Carefully. There's no one-size-fits-all answer to the question of whether or not a gift is in order.

If you think you'd like to send a gift, then it's probably the thing to do.

"The manner of giving is worth more than the gift," says a character in Pierre Corneille's play, "Le Menteur." . . . Great grace may go with a little gift; and precious are all things that come from friends," wrote Theocritus.

Follow the advice of these purveyors of wisdom and:

- Keep the price small but consider your selection carefully, so that when the gift arrives, the recipient will know immediately it was chosen especially for him or her.

- Present your gift with style but without regard to the dollar value. Of course, if you know you can afford a more expensive gift, by all means spend the money.

At the same time, don't feel bad if the recipient must decline the gift. Permit the individual to do so without a protest from you. It's then that you tender the gift of understanding.

CHOOSING TASTEFUL GIFTS

If you're going to send a gift because you want to, then there's a good reason for it. Let this reason be your guide in selecting the gift. If, for example, you had difficulty learning the new computer software system and spent lunch hours on the telephone getting support from an expert who missed lunches to counsel you, treat him to lunch.

Contact his secretary and confirm that he doesn't have a lunch appointment, then arrange with a gourmet lunch emporium to prepare a fine meal, place it in a fancy lunch basket, and deliver it to his desk at noon. Ask them to include a note from you:

"Thanks for everything. Please be my guest for lunch. No interruptions. I promise. Jean."

Inform his secretary, so he doesn't slip out unexpectedly. Voila! This is literally a tasteful gift!

Not Too Personal, Please

Personal gifts that reflect your knowledge of what someone enjoys are appropriate. Be sure, however, that your selections aren't too personal. That kind of gift doesn't belong in the business setting and you'll breach etiquette standards.

A gift certificate that entitles the recipient to shop at a fine clothing store may be an appropriate gift while a gift of lingerie you selected from that store is not. On the other hand, mailing a one-pound tin of a favorite pipe tobacco to a colleague qualifies as a personal gift but doesn't exceed reasonable limits.

Your boss arrives at work wearing a smart new fuchsia-colored raincoat. You admire the unusual color and tell her so. A few days later, while shopping, you see an umbrella that matches her coat. You purchase it and hold it at the office to present to her the next rainy day.

If you do establish a pattern of gift-giving when there's no special occasion, you can present a greeting card or a handshake and some words of cheer on those occasions when others are engaged in gift-giving activity. You may find this approach to gift-giving more joyful for you and the recipient.

As you can see, it's not difficult to follow the guidelines suggested by the quotations cited above.

When you join others in presenting a gift, you may not be able to adhere to these guidelines as carefully as you do when you're the sole gift-giver. Owing to combined contributions, the dollar value of the gift will be greater. Still, you can do your best to see to it that the gift is not a generic kind of gift and that it's presented with grace and style.

A Gift for Someone You Don't Know

You may be invited to the wedding of your coworker's son or to a housewarming party at the home of the company president. You wouldn't attend either function without bringing a gift but the normal approach to gift selection can't be applied since you don't know the people who will receive the gift.

One option is to attend the function first and select and mail the gift later. In the case of a housewarming, you'll have an opportunity to see the house and meet the host or hostess before you select a gift. Plan to send the gift no more than two or three days after the event. It can be delivered along with your thanks for your host's and hostess's gracious hospitality.

In the case of a wedding, you may want to ask if the couple registered with a bridal registry. This is a list of the couple's preferences that is on file at a well-known store. If you don't care for using the bridal registry, inquire about the couple. Will they live together in a house or an apartment? Is their lifestyle casual or formal? Questions that help you get to know the couple will help you decide on a gift. Of course, you may select a typical wedding gift (e.g., crystal vase, candlesticks). Sometimes it's the only reasonable option. It's considerate to be sure the couple has exchange privileges in case you purchase something they receive several of. To make this possible, you'll want the gift box to contain the name and address of the store where the gift was purchased. If necessary, ask the sales clerk to place the store's business card in the box.

DELIVERY: IN PERSON OR BY MAIL?

There are times when gift delivery in person is out of the question owing to logistics. You're not there! You may, however, arrange to have a gift delivered even though you'll be attending a function or sharing time with the individual for whom the gift is intended. A flower arrangement that you expect to be used as a centerpiece for a dinner party should be delivered shortly before guests arrive. As a matter of fact, most floral gifts are best left for the florist to deliver. Careful care and handling help flowers and plants reach their destination in peak condition. Other perishable items (i.e., fine cheeses and fancy fruits, freshly prepared chocolates, baked goods) also benefit from careful care and handling. Whenever possible, arrange to have your supplier deliver them.

Remember, "The manner of giving is worth more than the gift." If, for example, your dinner-party hostess is unaware of your intention to supply the floral centerpiece for the table, she'll probably obtain a centerpiece on her own. If, however, you notify her in advance or arrange for the florist to notify her and ask her about color preferences, your gift becomes more valuable. Don't arrange for freshly baked cakes, fully ripened fancy fruits, or similar foodstuffs to arrive at your host's door without advance notice, either. Since the host typically spends time, energy and dollars to arrange for desserts, this surprise gift would represent a challenge rather than a welcome addition to the meal.

Say, "I've arranged for three Oscar's gourmet cheesecakes to be delivered to your home on Saturday around four o'clock. I wanted to be sure this meets with your approval and to let you know you needn't concern yourself about refrigeration since the cakes will be delivered late in the day and should be held at room temperature for a few hours before serving."

Attention to Details

"We find great things are made of little things . . . " wrote Robert Browning. Your attention to gift-giving details is an important part of your business etiquette.

Does this surprise you?

If it comes as a surprise to many in your circle of business acquaintances, then it permits you to be a leader! Think through the gift process from selection to delivery, including making sure it's possible for someone to exchange the gift or to anticipate the arrival of a gift that's intended for immediate use, and you'll get a reputation for being thoughtful, considerate of others, a nice person. As a matter of fact, you'll embody all the fine qualities that make others feel comfortable with you and therefore want to work with you and for you.

Here's my gift for you

When a business associate presents a wrapped gift, it's appropriate to open it as soon as possible. Since a gift generally delights the recipient, the gift-giver will want to share in your pleasure when you learn what the package contains.

If you're busy greeting many guests and receive many gifts, it's not possible to unwrap gifts, too. Put gifts aside for safe-keeping and give them your attention later.

If the occasion is a retirement party or a bridal or baby shower, most party-goers will expect to see the gifts. The comments which accompany the unwrapping of gifts add to the pleasure of the occasion and serve to entertain everyone. If, however, the occasion is a wedding or a graduate school graduation, or a more formal or solemn occasion, the gifts are generally opened after guests have departed.

SAYING THANK YOU WITH PANACHE

When you thank someone, put the focus on him or her first, and you last. Avoid saying, "Oh, you shouldn't have." Always specifically mention the gift item. This is especially important when you've received numerous gifts at the same time. A gift-giver likes to be assured you know which gift he or she selected for you. Here are some sample words of thanks:

"You chose something I always wanted but would never buy for myself. You're so perceptive. Thank you!"

"Where did you find this zim-a-gig? You're so observant. This will make mail-opening chores a breeze. Thanks so much."

"Leave it to you to supply the flowers for the table. Not only were they lovely, I appreciated having one less thing to do to get ready for the party. You're very considerate. Thanks."

When you write a thank-you note, it should sound as though you are saying it. Keep the thank-you note short and to the point and send it as soon as possible after you receive a gift.

If you've received numerous gifts, you really must take the time to acknowledge them as soon as possible, too. A personal message is in order for each one. If you're sending thanks for a wedding gift, gift-givers should recognize you left for a honeymoon trip immediately after the reception and won't expect to hear from you until shortly after you return.

Bereavement

After you send flowers to a funeral home when a coworker's parent dies, you may later receive a printed thank-you message from the family. This is one occasion for which the omission of a personal message can be excused. Still, it's a warmer communication when it contains a sentence or two that's handwritten:

"Your kindness is especially meaningful to me in this time of sorrow."

"The time you spent with me and my family during this difficult time is appreciated."

"In times of sorrow, the support of friends and colleagues helps ease the pain. I thank you for reaching out to me."

You should never be too busy or too distracted to take the time to thank someone for his or her gift or display of kindness.

In the business world, where the clock often appears to race twice as fast as anywhere else, small acts of kindness and gracious manners usually make a deep and lasting impression.

There may be times when others don't appear to appreciate your efforts on their behalf. They are the ones who are lacking in savoir faire, not you. Don't adopt an "if you can't beat 'em, join 'em" approach. Do the "right thing" because you refuse to do anything less.

10

Introductions

Who are you?

Who am I?

Let's find out and let's give each of us a chance to shine. After all, we're out here in the business world where there's a keen need to know who is who.

If you develop a facility for remembering people's names, you'll find that making introductions is practically painless. Of course, there are times when you'll introduce people you have not met before to one another and times when, try as you may, you'll forget a name. Don't permit any of your concerns to keep you from making introductions. If you approach people with confidence, a smile, and a positive manner, they'll usually help you out. Moreover, you're practicing good business etiquette when you help business people to become acquainted with one another. When you represent the host company, it's downright rude to let someone hang on the edge of the crowd. Welcome him and invite him into the circle. Even when your company isn't hosting the gathering, *Everyday Business Etiquette* strategy urges you to take the lead when it comes to making others feel comfortable. You shouldn't move in on your host and take over his or her duties but you shouldn't permit a potential customer, client, or associate to stand around feeling lost. And if you're the individual standing at the edge of the crowd, move into the circle and introduce yourself.

"I'm Bob Rengle. I see from your name tag that you're Phil Whisk. Nice to meet you Phil."

"I'm Bob Rengle. Are you attending the Blakely Seminar? Me, too. May I ask your name?"

WHO IS INTRODUCED FIRST?

There is an accepted order to making introductions. It helps to know it although in some circles the order may be disregarded. As a result, you're on safe ground if you use these guidelines but you shouldn't judge others to be out of bounds if they don't comply. Things have changed; today's business climate is different than it was in the recent past.

As more and more two-paycheck households emerged, youngsters missed some opportunities, not the least of which was instruction regarding courtesy. When the youngsters eventually grew up and entered the work force, many learned what they'd missed. They enrolled in workshops and programs that spotlight courtesy. Others are out and about doing the best they can. They're unaware there's an established order and form.

People from different cultures and backgrounds mingle, and though some struggle to learn each other's rules, others stick with their own customs because they're uncomfortable with customs in the arena in which they find themselves working.

Here are four guidelines for making introductions.

- **A man is introduced to a woman.** "Ms. Sands, allow me to introduce Mr. Avery." Or, "Barbara Sands, allow me to introduce Sam Avery." If you don't know either individual well or if you believe each individual tends to be formal, or it's a serious business occasion, introduce them using the "Mr." or "Ms." before each name. Leave it to the individuals to request a first-name basis. (i.e., "Please, call me Barbara.")

- **A child is introduced to an adult.** "Mr. Carlysle, I would like you to meet my nephew, Todd Right." If Todd Right is a young adult, you can refer to him as Mr. Todd Right. You need not mention Mr. Carlysle's first name if he is some years Todd's senior or if Carlysle holds an executive position and Todd is relatively new to the workplace or not yet employed. In effect, you alert Todd to refer to Carlysle as Mr. Carlysle.

Carlysle may say, "Frank Carlysle. Good to meet you," as he extends his hand for a handshake.

This form helps to demonstrate respect for someone's experience and achievements. You'll use the same form to introduce a junior executive to a senior executive.

- **A junior executive is introduced to a senior executive.** When you're making introductions within the company, you'll say, "Mr. Senior executive,

I'd like to introduce Mr. Junior executive." It may be that the senior executive is years younger than the junior executive. The order of the introduction (who is introduced to whom) honors an individual's experience and achievements, not age. He or she "receives" the person who is less accomplished in the business environment.

- **Anyone is introduced to a guest of honor.** "Celebrity" Smith, I'd like to present our company president, Carlo Conti." While the guest of honor "receives" the company president, at the same time you have honored the company president by including his business title in the introduction process.

Fine-Tuning Form

These guidelines can be adapted to virtually any circumstances. If who is to be introduced to whom is uncertain, determine which person is more firmly established in the environment where the introduction is taking place. If you invite a company executive to your home for dinner, and your parents are there, you'll introduce the executive to your parents rather than introduce your parents to her. In your home environment, your parents are the established people and it's courteous to permit them to "receive" your colleague. "Mary and Charles Valley, Mom and Dad, I'd like to introduce Tarisha Poole."

An easy way to remember: Use the name of the "most special" person first:

- Woman (introducing man to a woman): Mary, I'd like you to meet . . ."
- Adult (introducing child to an adult): "Mr. Carlysle, I'd like you to meet . . ."
- Guest of honor (introducing anyone to guest of honor): "Celebrity, I'd like you to meet . . ."
- Most deserving person(s) [introducing anyone to deserving person(s)]: "Mom and Dad, I'd like you to meet . . ."

SAMPLE LETTERS OF INTRODUCTION YOU CAN USE

It's not uncommon to correspond with a colleague for purposes of making an introduction. The letter may be hand-delivered by the individual who wants to be introduced or, more likely, sent by mail just prior to the person's arrival. If you elect to use a very short form, you'll give your business card to someone and pen a note on the card: "This is to introduce John Pike."

If you write a letter of introduction, it should be easy to compose. If you say what you mean and mean what you say, because your sentiments are heartfelt, the letter will be useful. If you're asked to write a letter and you feel disinclined to do so, but feel you can't comfortably decline, you may want to use the business-card approach.

A letter of introduction won't be any less well received when sent electronically. Feel free to transmit the introduction by fax or speed it along using electronic mail.

"Keep It Short and Simple." This rule may challenge your writing ability, but when you use the KISS approach, you demonstrate consideration for the reader's time.

Blaise Pascal wrote:

> *"Je n'ai fait celle-ci plus longue que parce que je n'ai pas eu le loisir de la faire plus courte."*
> *I have made this letter longer than usual, only because I have not had the time to make it shorter."*
>
> (*Lettres Provinciales,* 1657)

If you agree to write a letter of introduction, take the time to do the job short!

If you ask someone to write a letter of introduction on your behalf, and you feel comfortable asking for a brief letter, do so. It's more likely to be read.

Here are some sample written introductions you may want to adapt:

Dear Claire:

When I learned that Elaine Clark was Seattle-bound, I urged her to contact you without delay. Elaine is an accomplished concert pianist and is moving to Seattle to accept a position with the Seattle Philharmonic Orchestra. She will arrive in town on or about September 10th with your office telephone number in her hand!

Elaine tells me that in addition to performances with the Orchestra she will seek outside concert engagements. I indicated that if you're able to represent her, she'll be in capable hands and if you're unable to represent her, you can probably advise her on how best to proceed.

Elaine is the daughter of one of my closest business associates. Any courtesy you can extend to Elaine will be appreciated by those of us laboring here in Cleveland who have Elaine's best interests at heart.

Thanks so much.

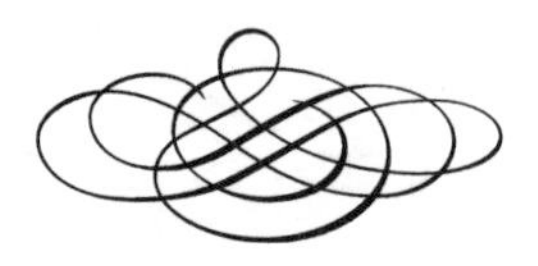

Dear Buck:

Mark Seiler is a skilled computer systems analyst whose quiet demeanor tends to camouflage his quick wit and on-target assessment of most situations. Those few of us who know him well are frequently exposed to this "other Mark" and feel the richer for it. When he asked me to contact you on his behalf, I applauded his good judgment, and take up my pen with pleasure.

Mark and his new bride, Betsy Clark, will move to Chicago at the end of May since Betsy has accepted a teaching position at the University.

I speak of you often and Mark is well aware of the enviable reputation you and your company enjoy in Chicago and throughout Illinois. Mark has received two bona fide job offers in the Chicago area and would like to confer with you regarding same. He knows you have a full schedule and assures me he can be brief and to the point. I know that if you're able, you'll contact Mark to establish a meeting time within the next few days. (His home telephone number and office number appear at the bottom of this page.)

I'll look forward to seeing you next month at convention time.

Sincerely,

Dear Mary:

Ms. Dawn Twichen has worked for my brother-in-law and his business associates for fourteen years. They are closing their local plant and attempting to assist nine employees to find new positions since these people aren't able to relocate with the company.

I'm writing to you on Ms. Twichen's behalf because she is both an extremely capable senior manager in a manufacturing environment and a fine person. I know how you pride yourself on hiring good people and thought I'd take this opportunity to notify you of these circumstances. I've taken the liberty of telling Ms. Twichen I am contacting you and she won't be surprised if you or someone in your personnel department contacts her to arrange for an interview.

As I send this note on its way, I feel certain I'm doing both you and Ms. Twichen a service by making this introduction. It pleases me to do so especially because you've done me a similar favor in the recent past.

Yours truly,

MASTERING USE OF SPECIAL TITLES

You may not be in the habit of associating with members of royalty, congresspeople, judges, and mayors on a regular basis, but you'll want to address them correctly when you occasionally write to them, introduce them to others, or speak with them directly. In addition to displaying your good manners and respect for their titled positions, your mastery of form should help to put everyone at ease. The titled persons should feel comfortable when you address them correctly and anyone else who may be introduced will feel guided by an expert (i.e., you) in the event he or she is unfamiliar with correct procedure.

Most business people have occasion to interact with practicing physicians, members of the clergy, and local law enforcement people or fire-department personnel on a more regular basis. You refer to Dr. Smones when your dentist seeks you out for business advice or Rabbi Rose when an official of the Jewish faith presides at ground-breaking ceremonies for a neighborhood youth center.

There's no reason to think that titles you use with less frequency or have not had occasion to use at all are more difficult to master than those with which you're familiar.

Dictionary Directions

A comprehensive dictionary contains far more information than most people expect to find on its pages. Many dictionaries contain forms of address. Check the Index in your dictionary and you should find titles and information regarding use. If, for example, you're writing a letter, you'll address an assembly member: The Honorable ———, Member of Assembly, and begin your letter with the words "Dear Sir:" or "Dear Madam:."

"The Honorable" is a title of respect which you can use to address someone but which is inappropriate for someone to use when referring to himself or herself.

Someone who has earned a Ph.D. may prefer to be called "Dr." or may not bother with the title. When you address this individual on paper, you'll use his or her name followed by the Ph.D. (for example, Gail Sanderson, Ph.D.) and proceed to write: "Dear Dr. Sanderson:"

If you know the person well and know she doesn't use her title, you'll dispense with it, too. Ms. Gail Sanderson. Dear Gail:. If you don't know the individual well but have been told she doesn't use her title, it's best to use it anyway until such time as she may confirm she prefers "Ms."

Today, it's not surprising to find that a woman holds a titled position (e.g., municipal court judge) while her husband does not. When you send correspondence to the couple, you'll use her title: The Honorable Nancy E. Daws and Mr. Jeffrey B. Daws. If both spouses hold titles, you'll use them both. The Honorable Nancy E. Daws and The Honorable Jeffrey B. Daws.

If you feel uncertain about how to proceed, contact the offices of the official(s) in advance. Most have able assistants who are more than willing to give you the information you seek. Find out:

- The person's exact title
- The spelling of name and title
- The correct written form
- The correct spoken form
- If a spouse is to be included, how the spouse should be addressed

Don't forget to thank the assistant for providing you with the correct information and don't be reluctant to say who you are and why you need the information. Your efforts to be correct and accord individuals the special consideration they are entitled to should be welcome news to the professionals who support them. Moreover, you'll feel your confidence level rise when you know you're well prepared.

11

Gratuities

TIPS ON TIPS THAT HELP YOU LOOK GOOD

Some view a tip as a small gift that helps to say, "thanks for a job well done." Others view a tip as an inducement awarded in hopes of good service next time they arrive at the location or of continuing good service during their current stay.

Since many service providers receive a minimum wage and depend upon gratuities to boost earnings, they view a tip as important and a good tip as most welcome. Most service providers remember customers who treat them generously and hasten to give those customers excellent service whenever an opportunity is presented.

All things considered, it makes good business sense to take good care of the people who service you regularly. You may decide that the 15 percent gratuity is sufficient for service providers you may never see again but a 20 percent gratuity is appropriate for the waiters and waitresses with whom you interact regularly. Whether you elect to leave a 15 percent or 20 percent gratuity, it's smart to treat all service providers with respect and let them know by your words and actions that you appreciate their service.

Everyday Business Etiquette philosophy directs that everyone deserves exposure to your good manners. So, whether it's your barber or hair dresser, a golf caddy, a taxi cab driver, a health club locker room attendant, or anyone else who normally receives a tip for service, be prepared to say, "please," "thank you," and "excuse me," when appropriate, in addition to leaving a tip.

Most people respond favorably to your courteous approach or response to them. You'll find almost any experience is more pleasant for you when you behave in a pleasant rather than a brusque manner.

People who take note of your behavior are likely to be favorably impressed by your display of good manners. You never know when your boss may be within earshot of your conversation with a delivery man who arrives at the reception center.

"You can't leave that here!" gets everyone's attention when you're loud and abrupt.

"Please wait. I'll call Customer Service to find out where this package is to be deposited. It will just take a moment," sounds better to everyone's ears.

When at some later date you're being considered for a promotion to a job where an even temperament is an asset, your pleasant reception-center behavior may prove to be that something extra which causes your boss to consider you the front runner for the position.

Don't feel bullied into leaving a monetary tip when service is poor but do remain calm. A loud or unpleasant confrontation with a discourteous or inept service provider detracts from the image you wish to project. In the long run you won't reform this individual and you stand to gain nothing. If you must vent your anger, do so by taking positive action. Make a vow to never return to this establishment or plan to contact the business owner and report the incident. It may be, however, that this action isn't worth your time.

WHO SHOULD LEAVE THE TIP?

When you're the host or hostess, you should leave the tip.

When you invite the boss to lunch but he or she insists on leaving the gratuity, you may want to graciously agree although you should be prepared to cover the bill and tip.

If you're the direct recipient of some service but you're someone's guest, you may leave a tip unless you're told that everything has been taken care of. If, for example, you're invited to your client's country club for dinner, you'll probably give the parking attendant a tip when he or she returns your car. You may also leave a tip with the individual who secures your hat and coat. You should not attempt to tip the dining room captain or table-service people. Don't attempt to force a gratuity on anyone who declines to accept it, since you may be asking them to break a trust with their employer or with your host or hostess.

When someone is to be your guest and may incur some small expenses like those just described, you may want to make arrangements and tell that individual that everything has been taken care of. If your guest is someone of modest means, it may tax his or her budget to handle tips at an elegant club. If your guest is visiting from another country, he or she may feel relieved not to have to tangle with the perplexities of what's appropriate. In either case, your generous hospitality should take the bumps out of the occasion and that's in everyone's best interest.

As a rule of thumb, whoever pays the bill also takes care of the tips. If the bill is shared, the cost of tips is shared, too.

HOW MUCH IS APPROPRIATE?

If you don't know how much money to tip or whether to tip, you're unprepared to perform well and may feel your composure slip when you're out and about with a client or someone you wish to impress. There are general rules you can follow but it's of enormous value to be alert to what the going rates are in the circles in which you conduct business. Don't hesitate to ask experienced colleagues about what's appropriate.

Tipping customs vary. In large cities or first class hotels and resorts you may want to choose a high-end gratuity from the suggested range (i.e., 15 to 20 percent). When a 15 percent gratuity is automatically added to your bill, which is the practice at some restaurants and other establishments, nothing more is necessary.

Common business tipping occasions and suggestions:

- Maitre d' or, captain: $10.00 for special service
- Waiter or waitress: 15 to 20 percent of the total bill
- Wine steward: 10 to 15 percent of the wine bill
- Washroom attendant: $.50 to $1.00
- Coat room attendant: $1.00 for one coat and $.75 for each additional coat or hat, minimum tip $1.00
- Parking valet: $2.00
- Taxi driver: 15 percent of total bill, not less than $.75
- Delivery person: $1.00
- Skycap/baggage helper: $1.00 minimum and $.50 for each additional bag
- Shoeshine: $1.00
- Doorman: No tip for holding door but $1.00 minimum for other service such as obtaining a taxi

Tip Computers International (TCI), San Diego, California [(800) 527-9493 or (619) 488-7332], publishes smaller-than-playing-card-size cards which list suggested amounts to tip and provide at-a-glance computations. The company's products are regularly featured in popular magazines and newspapers and TCI offers a chart with international tipping information, including a list of situations in which tipping isn't customary.

If you feel you must obtain more detailed information check your local library or book store for recent "tipping" titles and make a thorough study of the subject. The fact that such books are available suggests the business of tipping is a serious one. As you work to perfect your business etiquette acumen, you'll want to master tipping practices, too.

When you leave a tip, don't make a grand show of it. Leave the gratuity on the table, or in the hand, or tucked into a service provider's pocket with a light touch and no fanfare.

A LIST OF TIPS FOR SPECIAL TIPPING SITUATIONS

(1) You play golf with a client at a golf course he selects. He insists on paying and you're aware that he tips the golf caddies but doesn't tip the golf pro who spent time assisting each of you. You want to give the golf pro $20.00. Will you embarrass the client?

If you're discreet, you probably won't embarrass anyone and you'll be able to engage the golf pro next time without concern for what appears to be a breach of tip-etiquette. It's possible, however, that your client has tipped the pro and you're unaware of the exchange. You can say, "Jack, I want to thank you for everything and I insist that you let me take care of the golf pro's tip." He'll let you know then if he's already done that.

(2) A masseuse and masseur visit your offices once a week and the company covers the cost. If you take advantage of these services, must you provide a tip? If so, how much?

Yes. Twenty-five percent of the bill is not uncommon but since you probably don't know the cost, ask colleagues who already take advantage of these services what's appropriate.

(3) My partner insists it's not necessary to tip a rental limousine driver and that it's included in the cost. Is he right?

Probably not. It's customary to tip the chauffeur 15 to 20 percent of the rental fee. When you engage a limousine, ask the company representative if the driver's gratuity is included.

(4) Is it proper to put a waiter's tip on my credit card? I think that he must be penalized since the restaurant owner pays a percentage to the credit card company for this service.

Your question suggests you're especially sensitive to the true value of the tip and that's commendable. Even though it's proper to add a gratuity to the credit card tab, you'll probably feel better about leaving cash when you pay the bill with a credit card. (As to whether or not the waiter is penalized, probably not.)

(5) My boss is an opera buff and gave me and my husband tickets to attend an opera. Do we have to tip the usher?

No.

(6) I give the shoeshine man in our office building a generous gratuity at holiday time each year. My secretary tells me that he should be tipped $1.50 a shine, too. Isn't that too much?

Ask your secretary why $1.50 is recommended when $1.00 a shine is not uncommon. Listen. Then you decide if the higher tip is warranted.

(7) I buy groceries for our office kitchen twice a month. I give the clerk who carries the groceries to my car $2.00. My boss says, it's not necessary to tip the clerk. Should I stop tipping?

No. It's appropriate to tip the clerk and if you stop suddenly you suggest the service isn't satisfactory.

(8) I spend a lot of money to have my hair cut and styled and the person who takes care of me is the shop owner. I don't give her a tip. My friend tells me I'm cheap. Is this true?

No. It's not necessary to tip the owner of the shop. If someone else shampoos your hair, however, it's appropriate to tip that individual $1.00–$2.00.

(9) I ride a train to work and always exchange a few pleasant words with the train conductor. Would he think me out of line to offer him a tip?

It's not necessary. Moreover, once you tip an individual, it's difficult to stop the practice. If you want to use the end-of-year holidays as an excuse to tip the conductor, the gift should be appreciated.

(10) My health club instructor has a magnetic personality and I notice that some club members give him tips. Is this customary?

If you notice the practice of tipping the instructor is customary at your health club than the answer is yes. It isn't considered customary in other health clubs but that's of no consequence.

(11) I'm on a tight budget and can't afford to tip 20 percent for restaurant service. Does this mean, I shouldn't eat in restaurants?

If you can afford to pay the restaurant tab and include a 15 percent gratuity, you should feel comfortable about enjoying restaurant service. Your patronage helps to give the servers their jobs and there's no need to apologize for leaving a 15 percent tip. Words of praise, smiles, and your thanks are further ways to show your appreciation for excellent service.

(12) I tip my child's day care center supervisor at the end of work weeks when she stays a few extra minutes with my child because I've been detained. My husband says, it's part of her job and a tip isn't necessary.

Since you've already instituted the practice of tipping and it hasn't been declined, you're bound to continue the arrangement. If you're pleased with the care your child receives, the issue of a tip is basically a nonissue. When someone provides a special service, even though it may be considered part of the job it's thoughtful to supply a special gift or a tip.

(13) I left a 20 percent tip at a restaurant and later learned that management included a 15 percent gratuity when they presented the bill. I want to ask for reimbursement. Would this be tactless?

Yes. Consider the experience a learning experience and let it go at that.

(14) A customer handed me a tip when I carried office supplies from our store to her car. I own and operate the store and don't accept tips but the customer insisted I accept her tip. My partner told me she complained to him that I accepted the tip. What can I do?

Forget about it. If it happens again, thank her and tell her you'll donate the sum to a charity.

(15) When I dine with five or six coworkers, there's usually a prolonged discussion about who owes what. Some agree to a 15 percent gratuity and others want to pay 20 percent. What's the best way to handle this dilemma?

You're probably not the only one who feels uncomfortable about this climax to the occasion. Ask everyone to agree beforehand that one individual will pay the tab and a 15 percent gratuity. Then, ask someone to take charge. If appropriate, you can all give this person $10, $20 or a reasonable sum before you dine. He or she can reimburse individuals later, away from the restaurant. If this suggestion isn't satisfactory, ask coworkers to make suggestions.

12

Correspondence

ELECTRONIC CORRESPONDENCE

Unless you encrypt electronic messages (e.g., facsimile, electronic mail), the person you're writing to may not be the only one who will read the communication. As a result, you're acting discreetly when you refrain from putting sensitive information in writing. There are other do's and don'ts that help you maintain decorum and indicate to others you have a good command of correct procedure. The recent appearance of the word "netiquette" which is a reference to electronic networking etiquette, signals us that business people who use these modern-day communication tools are well aware there's a right way and a wrong way to proceed.

Review the following list and use information that's appropriate to your needs.

Do:

1. *Do identify your target person and yourself so that either one of you can be contacted. In addition to your fax number, you should provide a telephone number or address, or both.*

   John transposed numbers when he prepared a fax to be transmitted to a supplier. The fax number did, however, belong to an accountant. When the accountant's secretary received the communication she wasn't able to notify John about the error because John didn't provide adequate information. She certainly couldn't contact the supplier because the supplier's fax number was unknown. That's why the communication arrived at the accountant's office in the first place.

2. *Do write as though you're speaking to a person. If you're too cryptic or the message is abbreviated, the individual may get the wrong impression.*

   When Martin sent an as-soon-as-possible request to the warehouse manager at the distribution center in another city, he didn't receive the rapid response he anticipated. The manager was an efficient and capable person and Martin was puzzled. One week later, Martin got what he wanted via the U.S. Postal Service.

   What was Martin's message to the manager?

   "Mid-month widget inventory report required. Confidential transmission imperative. Accuracy essential. ASAP."

   As soon as possible is a vague reference and wasn't accuracy more important than speed? The instructions regarding "confidential transmission" were open to interpretation. The warehouse manager wasn't equipped to transmit coded figures electronically so chose to send the information by the postal service, a reasonable, albeit slower option.

3. *Take care to check spelling, grammar, and general appearance of your message. Just because you're using modern day technology doesn't mean you're at liberty to disregard old-fashioned form.*

4. *Be aware that small print may not transmit clearly and alert your contact to notify you if he or she has difficulty reading the data. If in doubt, perhaps you should use a messenger service or express mail to deliver the material. In either case, your thoughtfulness and think-ahead approach should be appreciated.*

5. *Include a message subject notation near the top of the communication. It gives your contact person an idea of what to expect and enables him or her to assign the message a priority. In a busy office, communications may not be read immediately. If you always describe your messages as high priority, your important messages won't have impact.*

Don't:

1. *Don't assume all requests you receive are bona fide. If in doubt, check it out!*

2. *Don't offend anyone. If you chuckled when you heard a tasteless pun, don't share it with your electronic mail contact via this forum. This person's assistant or someone else who will read the message may be offended by your remarks.*

3. *Don't type your message using all upper-case letters. Internet users call this "shouting" and claim it's difficult to read and tends to annoy recipients.*
4. *Don't forget that an established electronic mail shorthand exists. "Thanks in advance," for example, is communicated using TIA. "By the way," using BTW. If you're new to the scene and don't recognize the dozen or more abbreviations currently in use, don't accuse those who use them of being improper.*
5. *Don't forget to number the pages of a long fax message. This will make it easier for the recipient to keep order if he or she cuts the pages and clips them together for ease of handling when reading or filing.*

SELECTING APPROPRIATE STATIONERY

> *"The look you choose can be formal, casual, or somewhere in between. If you find a purple envelope with white polka dots on your desk in the morning, you don't expect it to contain compelling business information. As a matter of fact, if it's on the desk with a lot of important-looking envelopes, you'll probably open it last."*
>
> Marilyn Pincus, *Projecting a Positive Image* (Barron's, Hauppauge, NY, 1993)

When you select and use stationery that complements the message you're sending, you make it easier for the recipient to grasp the message. You're in step with *Everyday Business Etiquette* practices, since this is a considerate thing to do.

Take notice of printed materials that come across your desk and pay attention to paper's color, thickness, design, and size when you confer with the office supplies representative or your local stationery store operator. Since you've got to choose some stationery, take the time and trouble to pick out stationery that works for you.

WHEN A HANDWRITTEN MESSAGE IS REQUIRED

Remember the expression, "hi-tech, hi-touch?"

When electronic telephone systems, personal computers, and facsimile machines were newer in the workplace, people recognized that although the new technology had much to recommend it, it was oh-so impersonal. It's generally agreed that people thrive on human contact and there are times when nothing else will suffice.

A handwritten message is less than high-tech and more hi-touch than a message generated using high-speed electronics. If your handwriting skills are superb, the handwritten message you generate is attractive to look at, easy to read, and conveys special warmth. Even if your scrawl won't win prizes, if it's legible use it to add a personal touch to your message.

"Ah, yes, but it's quick and easy to use my typewriter or personal computer," you say. True. Still, there are times when quick and easy don't merit the highest priority.

When a colleague or acquaintance suffers a loss or must deal with a seemingly insurmountable challenge (i.e., death of a loved one, job dismissal, life-threatening illness or injury), you should pen your words of concern, condolences, or offer of assistance.

Note-size writing paper will enable you to keep the message brief and help you to expedite the mission.

Anytime you generate a message and prefer to inject it with personal warmth, use your pen to get the job done. Plan to handwrite notes that:

- Congratulate someone
- Say thank you
- Extend an informal invitation
- Refuse a gift (because of company policy)

When you're one of several people at the office signing a store-bought greeting card, why not add a line or two along with your signature? Even when the greeting card verse is poignant, your personal thought added in your handwriting adds fervor to the message you wish to convey.

RESPONDING TO CORRESPONDENCE IN A TIMELY MANNER

Acknowledgment delayed is acknowledgment denied. That's one way to view the consequences of taking too long to notify someone who expects a response from you.

If you correspond with an old college friend who lives 2,000 miles away and you occasionally permit her latest letter to collect dust while it sits on your desk waiting for a reply, she'll forgive you. When you finally write and tell her whether you enjoyed the seminar you attended, purchased that used automobile you wrote about, or traded in your glasses for contact lenses, she'll be pleased to hear from you.

When you receive an invitation from a professional organization to serve on a special panel, when your boss and her husband invite the office staff to spend a weekend at their beach house, when a colleague sends electronic mail and suggests you spend Wednesday afternoon reviewing company archives together in preparation for a new marketing campaign, you had better respond in a timely fashion, or else! Or else, you invite their wrath. Wouldn't these folks earn your wrath if the shoe were on the other foot and you were the one waiting for a reply? Yes!

Plan to respond to all invitations within twenty-four hours of receipt. If you're unable to determine whether you're able to accept the invitation and must obtain information (e.g., review flight information, make child-care arrangements, determine whether your boss is agreeable to your time spent away from the office) before you can respond, it may be appropriate to let the other person know that you'll need time before you can respond. Ask yourself if your delay in responding with certainty will inconvenience the person who extended the invitation. If so, decline.

When you receive an invitation that asks you to respond by a specific date, honor that request. Ignoring it constitutes a serious breach of good manners.

GREETINGS AND SALUTATIONS

"To whom it may concern," is a rather cold and dreary salutation although it is certainly a polite one. When you sit down to write, do your best to find out precisely who the letter should be targeted to so you can "salute" that individual appropriately:

- Dear Mr. Chapman:
- Dear Philip:
- Dear Editor:
- Dear Director:
- Dear Chairperson:

Write your opening paragraph so that it "hooks" your reader. If you can do that, your correspondence should be read and the business of business will progress.

Use proper grammar and punctuation. A colon follows the salutation in a business or more formal greeting while a comma follows the salutation in a personal greeting. Proper grammar builds a strong foundation for good manners in your correspondence. If the reader is distracted by misspelled words or other mistakes, the message loses impact. Moreover, a sloppy letter can be insulting. "Why are you wasting my time with this mess?"

The English language is not an easy language to master, but if you work at it, you'll raise your communication skills to new heights.

Here are some opening sentences designed to "hook" the reader. Do you understand why?

"How do busy people like you and Sally find time to entertain folks at your vacation home, too? Don't tell me! Just permit me to accept with pleasure your kind invitation for the weekend of July 10."

The focus is on the reader and he's being complimented, too. Of course, he's hooked!

"Your ability to recognize talented people is as keen as your ability to serve fine wines. It was a pleasure to meet your protégé, Mark Willeston, at your club on Friday. As I write to thank you again for your hospitality, let me take the opportunity to tell you that Mark has an appointment to meet with our human resources director next Monday."

The reader's good judgment is validated and he's being kept in the information loop. Of course, he'll read on!

"You were sorely missed at our industry trade show in Atlanta last month. Several of my customers expressed an interest in your services. I've taken the liberty of listing their names and telephone numbers below:"

The reader is delighted to have been missed and gratified to learn of an opportunity for new business. Not only will he read on, he'll probably pick up the telephone to call those on the list without delay.

ABBREVIATION KNOW-HOW

Send your correspondence to AZ when you want to send it to Arkansas and you're in trouble. Someone in Arizona will be the recipient even if it's an employee of the U.S. Postal Service.

That's a glaring misuse of an abbreviation but there are others and none of them enhance your correspondence.

- Academic degrees are frequently abbreviated following an individual's name (e.g., Ph.D., M.D., or M.A.). If an individual has earned more than one degree, take care to position them in the order of importance, saving the most important degree for last.

- When addressing a Reverend you may use the abbreviation Rev. but it should be used with the lady's or gentleman's full name: Rev. James T. Paulson as opposed to Rev. Paulson. Rev. J. T. Paulson is permissible.
- If you're writing to Martin Q. Crane Jr., you'll want to avoid placing a comma at the end of the last name and before the abbreviation Jr. Martin Q. Crane, Jr., for example, is considered incorrect in spite of the fact that it's in common usage.

How does anyone always know what's correct?

Check with the experts.

Obtain a copy of *The Elements of Style* by William Strunk Jr. and E. B. White and *The Elements of Grammar* by Margaret Shertzer or other grammar handbooks. Keep them nearby as you write. Consult them. Your use of abbreviations, punctuation, and style will be correct and your goal to deliver eminently readable and correct correspondence will be achieved.

If you deduce that being grammatically correct is a lifelong pursuit, you're absolutely right!

A TEN-POINT CHECKUP FOR YOUR CORRESPONDENCE

1. *Is the letter necessary? Don't send a letter unless it's the best way to accomplish your goal. The opening paragraph should "hook" the reader's attention. Does it?*
2. *Is the message easy to understand and as brief as possible? Many professional writers are fond of saying, "less is more." If your letter doesn't fit on one page, it may be too long.*
3. *Make sure you've correctly spelled the intended recipient's name and used the proper title. When a business title or special position (i.e., Esq., C.P.A.) should be acknowledged, use correct form. Steven H. Shenando, Esq. is the correct way to address an envelope addressed to an attorney, not Mr. Steven H. Shenando, Esq. When in doubt, telephone Mr. Shenando's office and ask his secretary for clarification.*

   If you haven't corresponded with an individual for some time, he or she may no longer have the same title. Ask.

4. *Is there sufficient "white space?" When correspondence looks cluttered owing to lack of margin space, it may not be read or read with care.*

5. *Stationery should complement the message. Does it? If you're trying to convey a serious message, the paper and envelope shouldn't convey a playful image. No stripes, polka dots, or wild colors, please. No unusual shapes or printed graphics that don't support the impression you intend.*

6. *Did a real person sign the letter? A message that's signed "Quality First Team," or "The Advisory Committee" doesn't have clout. Take responsibility for the correspondence and sign the letter with your first and last name. The recipient will know precisely who to contact should he or she wish to respond.*

7. *If you used a second page of the letter solely for the purpose of signing the letter, toss it out. Edit the letter so that it fits onto one page or add to the letter, so that the final page contains something more than a Yours truly, Sincerely, or Best wishes, along with a signature.*

8. *Examine punctuation and grammar. Are there too many or too few commas? If you asked a question, did you use a question mark? Does a new paragraph convey a new thought? Let a modern grammar handbook be your guide.*

9. *Recheck facts or figures for accuracy.*

10. *If the letter promises to include other material, that material should be ready to go.*

13 Telephone Communications

Someone who is rude to you over the telephone, in person or by recording can make you want to scream. Someone who displays good manners and says all the right things is a pleasure to know.

Even if you've been accustomed to telephone communications since you were a wee thing, take care to review your style and make sure to smooth over any rough edges that may have developed with time. It can happen!

ABCs OF PROPER OFFICE TELEPHONE GREETINGS

When someone arrives at your door, you typically welcome the individual, invite him or her to enter your office and offer a comfortable chair.

A caller who arrives by telephone should get virtually the same treatment.

Welcome a caller by clearly identifying yourself or your company so the person knows he or she has come to the right place.

Invite the person to proceed by paying careful attention to what he or she has to say.

Make the caller comfortable by demonstrating that you can be of assistance or direct the caller to someone who can be of assistance. Don't make your exit until you know the caller is being served.

These are the ABCs of an office telephone greeting. It's truly elementary and yet in today's complicated business world it's often an elusive goal. If you want to demonstrate your facility with business etiquette, check telephone procedures in your office now. What happens to a caller? Do you know?

Is a caller welcomed by a menu of options such as the following?

If you know your party's extension, press it now. If you need to place an order or require account information, press the number nine followed by the star key. Please, have your 22-digit account number ready. If you need information about the company's new products acquired via the Brown and Company merger, dial (800) 931-4321. If you want this message repeated, dial 8, followed by the pound key. If you do not have a touch-tone telephone, remain on the line until this recording cycles five times and an operator will assist you. Your telephone call is very important to us. We are experiencing an unusually heavy load of incoming calls and we ask that you do not hang up so that your call can be handled in the order in which it was received. Have a nice day!

Is this the kind of welcome someone gets when calling you or trying to reach someone at your company? Or perhaps, a harried telephone operator takes the call and says, "Can you wait, pl . . ." She then dashes off before finishing her question and doesn't know whether or not you can wait. When she finally transfers you to the incoming line of the person you desire to speak with, you find you've reached the person's voice mail. You must leave a message or dial 7, followed by a B, to reach an assistant. You dutifully follow those directions only to find the assistant's voice mail is waiting to record your every wish.

Is this the stuff that screams are made of?

You bet it is.

It's rude treatment, at best, and you don't want your callers exposed to it.

Still, if you don't monitor your telephone greeting from time to time it can "advance" into some variation of the above theme. Stick to the ABCs and your callers can save their screams for times when they're sitting in the audience at a horror movie.

WAYS TO END CONVERSATIONS WITH LONG-WINDED CALLERS

When you tell someone, "My secretary is signaling me that I have an important call waiting," or, "I really must leave for a meeting in two minutes," you're relying on some of the sage advice offered by telephone etiquette gurus over the last several years. The only problem is that if your caller has been exposed to that advice, too, he or she is "on" to you.

As a result, what you consider to be a tactful way to end a conversation with someone who doesn't know when to quit, can insult the person: "That so-and-so is just trying to get rid of me. What a nerve!"

Accordingly, it's time for a new and different approach to end conversations with long-winded callers.

Here's how:

- Help to guide a person so he or she can get to the point: "What is it you believe I can do to help?"

- Help the caller to simplify information: "Please, use short sentences. I'd like to take notes."
- Establish a time-frame for action: "Can you give me an exact date or time when this (mention the specific thing) must be completed?"

In short, guide the caller to reveal: who, what, why, when, and where. Then, make a judgment. Let the caller know what you'll do and when. This should effectively end the conversation. Here are some conversation enders:

"Let me consider what you've said and call you on Friday."

"Our general manager is probably the person who can assist you but, I'll find out and either he or I shall call you later today."

"I'm putting an information packet in the mail to you. After you review it, please, call my secretary to set up an appointment for a telephone conference. Then, we'll both be able to give this matter our undivided attention."

"I can't talk with you at length just now. Will it be convenient if I call you around 8:30 tomorrow morning?"

"It's clear to me that I can't assist you. There's no point in either of us spending any more time on this matter."

When Someone Is Rude—Or Worse

A caller who misrepresents himself or herself (e.g., claims to be Sam Brown's brother-in-law and you know Sam doesn't have one), attempts to obtain sensitive information (e.g., wants to know the age of the office security system), or behaves in any questionable manner whatsoever (e.g., uses offensive language) can be cut off without ceremony. Since there's no need to exercise good manners but only good judgment, hang up.

TAKING MESSAGES FOR OTHERS

When someone takes a telephone message for you, you want to know who called and when. It may help to know why, where, or what, too. You should obtain this information for others when you take messages for them. You exercise good business etiquette when you make sure you're:

Accurate. Get a complete name. Spell it correctly. Jot down the telephone number and if possible the time when the caller expects to be available.

Timely. Deliver the message as soon as possible. Let the person know there was a telephone call and don't assume he or she will notice the message you left on his or her desk.

Put the caller at ease, too. Let the person know you'll give a message to your associate as soon as he or she is available. Take care to maintain professional stature when providing the caller with information. You may want to say your associate is attending a seminar and isn't due back at the office until late afternoon. But it's not appropriate to discuss the seminar's topic, the location, or provide details. There's nothing to be gained and you may say more than you should and cause your associate some hardship. Exercise the four B's. Be polite. Be friendly. Be professional. Be cautious.

Another "B" to remember:

Be responsive. When you promise to return a call, keep your promise. New Jersey-based illustrator and cartoonist Tom Kerr reminds us that not replying to letters and phone calls is nothing short of bad manners.

"It is a real bugaboo of my wife's and mine, and the practice is currently rife in our industries."

BEEPER INTERRUPTIONS AND OCCASIONAL ELECTRONIC INTRUSIONS

The cellular telephone and technological devices which keep you in the informational loop have benefits galore. If you own and operate such devices, you can probably list two or three benefits without trying hard. That's the up side. There is, however, a down side.

Cellular telephones and free-roaming beckoning tools can:

- interrupt a conversation in which you're currently engaged
- distract others who can't help but overhear your comments
- prevent you from giving your undivided attention to matters at hand because you anticipate a call. You're tethered to and at the mercy of these communications tools.
- make noise in an environment where noise is unwelcome. If, for example, you're attending a new computer software training program, beeps or buzzes constitute unwelcome noise.

Don't offend others by using these tools without regard to their effect. Arrange to be incommunicado, when appropriate. If the seminar you will attend on Wednesday is important, surely someone at the office can handle your responsibilities for a few hours. You can call for messages during lunch time or break time. In case of an emergency, seminar personnel will alert you. In other words, use the old-fashioned communication network when newer electronic devices may work against you. When you do, you're both courteous and considerate of others. Not only might you save yourself some embarrassing moments, you will restore a healthy measure of peace and tranquility into what can otherwise be a very hectic business day.

14
Other Languages, Other Niceties, Other Resources

How do you say "please" and "thank you" in French? Spanish? Japanese? Italian? Portuguese?

If you're doing business in a foreign country, will your command of that country's language enable you to be on your best behavior?

To arrive at a sound answer to this question, re-position it.

Will an English-speaking person who comes from a distant country to do business with you be letter perfect when it comes to exercising good business etiquette on your turf?

Probably not.

You'll have to know more than words or expressions in order to be able to act graciously when doing business with people from other countries. Still, obtaining even a rudimentary command of the language is a good place to start. The fact that you make an attempt to speak another language will be appreciated by others. Even when the language of business is the English language, occasions arise when some facility with the dominant, local language will permit you to act with confidence and permit the business of conducting business to proceed.

SPEAKING THE LANGUAGE

It's easy to obtain specific language vocabulary lists and phrase books that supply recommended comments which apply to common situations. It's not easy, however, to memorize everything. Therefore, you'll need to customize learning to meet your needs. Consider your specific itinerary and list the phrases you may need in English. For example, you may need to say, "Can a hotel representative who speaks English assist me? I want to make arrangements to entertain guests in the hotel dining room."

What phrases will you need to use a telephone? How will you express some pleasantries to a business associate's non-English-speaking spouse (i.e., "It's a pleasure to meet you. You have a lovely home.")

Once you establish your list, locate the words and phrases you need and spend time memorizing those phrases.

The glossary of *Business in Mexico, Managerial Behavior, Protocol, and Etiquette* by Candace Bancroft McKinniss and Arthur A. Natella, Jr. (Binghamton, NY: Haworth, 1994) includes a basic business vocabulary list. Here you'll find the Spanish words and phrases for English words and phrases, including

- to buy on time . . . c*omprar a plazos*
- silent partner . . . *comanditario*
- to guarantee . . . *garantizar*

as well as general vocabulary words including

- *ancianos* . . . highly respected village elders
- *barrio* . . . a neighborhood of a city or town, usually with a church and plaza of its own

It's easy to see how this specific information can come in handy. Moreover, when you narrow your personal learning assignment to meet specific needs and establish reasonable priorities, you're not likely to feel overwhelmed.

Consider, too, how others may respond to what you'll say and try to familiarize yourself with key words that may be expressed in response to your questions and comments (e.g., "Nice to meet you," "I can't help you," "I'll call someone who can help you").

This do-it-yourself approach may suffice if you're traveling with others who have command of the language or you know that foreign business associates speak your language and that your language is spoken at the hotel and other places you expect to be. It can't be overly stressed, however, that when you make an attempt to learn some of the other person's language and use it, you inject a healthy measure of goodwill into the affiliation, and that is a basic tenet of *Everyday Business Etiquette* practices.

If you're going to conduct business abroad routinely or actually take up residence in a foreign country for a period of time, your needs will be different. You may enroll in formal classes to learn the necessary language, engage a tutor, purchase a comprehensive home-study language course which provides audio and reading material or you may do all three!

Using an Interpreter

When you conduct business with people who don't speak your language and you don't speak their language, or if all parties concerned have only a minimal grasp of what the other is saying, you'll avail yourself of the services of a translator.

Be aware that a skilled translator will want to prepare for the visit, too. This professional should have an understanding of your relationships with those with whom you'll spend time and be aware of your expectations.

According to Izumi Suzuki, a professional interpreter in the United States and Japan since 1973, it's important to understand the spin of communications.

> *"Spin may be defined as the flavor imparted to communications by innuendo, choice of phrases, tone, pace, pitch, or pause. Even so-called literal interpretations have a spin imparted by the dictionary used and schedule. For example, joking in America and silence in Japan can clearly signal to native speakers respectively anger or aggression or both. Without some spin, true meaning transfer through interpreting is doomed. As for the client, valuable information can be gained regarding the relative position of their counterparts and their personal relationships. Therefore, we serve our clients best by asking what spin they desire."*
>
> An Interpreter's Checklist, ATA *Chronicle*
> (American Translators Association) March 1995

Significant preparation will be necessary if you're to practice the art of business etiquette while doing business with people from other countries. This chapter has been designed to offer you food for thought and a rich supply of resource data. You can narrow down your broad understanding of what's desirable to obtain specific information that will permit you to do your job.

In brief, you'll focus on form and function, function and form, in the same way you do with all business relationships. The difference is that you can't rely upon a wealth of lifetime experiences for support. You know, for example, how to read and interpret body language when dealing with people whose ways are familiar to you. You don't know how to read and interpret body language when dealing with people whose ways are unfamiliar to you. Accordingly, preparation for business encounters with people from different countries may be perceived as more demanding. As one well-seasoned business seminar leader likes to tell her audiences about achieving any business goals, "put some zip in the trip." She puts lots of energy into the delivery of the word "zip" to emphasize that mobilizing personal energy to achieve goals helps individuals to be the best they can be. So, while you're focusing on demands, focus on putting zip into your trip!

Be Aware of Your Own Business Style

How does self-knowledge permit you to have more satisfying interactions with business people in other countries?

If, for example, you and your associates consider time a valuable commodity, might your counterparts in another country, who have a different assessment regarding the value of time, think of you as impatient, anxious, pushy?

This kind of them-and-us examination supports you as you work to build a strong foundation from which to move forward. Should you remain oblivious to differences it will be like rowing upstream without an oar. Difficult!

Since 1963, Prudential Relocation Intercultural Services (PRIS), in Boulder, Colorado, has provided a broad range of services for businesses. They conduct cross-cultural and language training programs focusing on over ninety countries for many of the Fortune 500 companies.

Gary M. Wederspahn, vice president of PRIS Global Services is the author of the article "Do You Know Your Cultural Identity?" (*Mobility*, July 1995). Mr. Wederspahn suggests that it's important to "know thyself" before you can work successfully with those who come from different cultures:

Regarding directness, he says:

> *"Don't beat around the bush," and "Tell it like it is!" Our country values simple, direct verbal and written communication. Those who are indirect are likely to be viewed with suspicion, as if they have something to hide or are lacking in self-confidence. However, in other countries, our directness may be perceived as bluntness to the point of rudeness.*

Regarding the American belief in egalitarianism (human equality, he says):

Our tendency to use our boss's first name, challenge authority easily, and expect equal treatment reveals a low power distance value. Cultures with high power distance frequently take our egalitarianism as an unwillingness to show proper deference and respect to those who deserve it.

You're probably beginning to understand that dealing with people from other countries requires:

- Some command of the language
- Awareness and control of communications spin
- Knowing your style and the other person's style of relating and doing business

There's More!

As one Whirlpool Corporation executive states, "Today's global players—including Whirlpool—need to encourage their employee teams to go much farther than simply embracing proper manners and etiquette."

Barbara Welke, the person in charge of Whirlpool's Partnership for Excellence program (a training program targeted to all levels of management) was asked why it's important to "think globally" rather than simply focus on good business etiquette when preparing to do business with people in other countries. She made several observations:

- Initiating change and leading change is not an easy thing to do. It means opening yourself up to having the way you've always done things questioned. You may have to concede that the way you do things is right for you but maybe not right for the other person. You need to "let go of it" and listen.
- Recognize that just because something wasn't invented in the United States doesn't mean it's not good. The tendency to embrace mine-is-best beliefs can get in the way unless you're alert and avoid it. Just because it didn't come from here doesn't mean it isn't something you can't grab hold of and run with.

Ms. Welke claims it's easier to make progress in the short term when you appreciate long-term benefits. If, for example, your company's financial health and well-being depends upon global success, so does your job! You obviously have an immediate interest in "thinking globally."

For those who attend face-to-face meetings, here are some further observations:

- Speak clearly and slowly and look at the person while you're speaking. If you're at a meeting table and turn your head to speak to the person seated next to you, chances are many others at the table won't see your face and will find it difficult to understand you. (Remember, many people speak English as a second language but need adequate time to translate and digest comments.)
- Select the models or metaphors you use with care. Baseball examples, for example, may not make sense to someone who lives in a country where baseball receives little attention. Make sure your "word pictures" can be translated—literally.
- Be realistic about timing when you build your agenda. When you're setting up a meeting schedule, for example, you may have to explain something three times and will need sufficient time to do so. If someone must read a document, the person is reading and translating and that takes more time.

If you go into the meeting feeling as though you'll cover so much in the first hour and move on to cover so much in the second hour, you're setting yourself up to become frustrated. Your feelings of frustration need no translation—they'll be obvious. So plan thoughtfully, and you'll be more successful.

NETWORKING WITH PEOPLE IN OTHER COUNTRIES

Of course, you may never have occasion to travel to another country to conduct business. Still, electronic communication systems or changes such as foreign ownership of your company or a supplier's company may link you with people who have different expectations than you have and who operate with a different set of rules. If you think they should shape their performance to suit your needs since they're working in your realm, you're permitting *Everyday Business Etiquette* goals to fade into the background. Take steps to boost your personal know-how and you'll be in a better position to keep business communications cordial, productive and profitable.

How to Do Business in Sixty Countries—Kiss, Bow or Shake Hands, (Boston: Bob Adams, 1994) by Terri Morrison, Wayne A. Conaway and George A. Borden offers an easy-to-read potpourri of information and provides answers to some of the following questions.

- Where is this person's country located on the planet? Are there mountains, oceans, deserts nearby?
- What are the neighboring countries? Is it easy to cross borders? Are the nations friendly toward one another?
- What's the climate like? Is it like the climate you experience?
- Is there a dominant religion? Language?
- What kind of food is favored? Dress style?
- Do people bicycle to work, own cars, use public transportation?
- Do people live in apartments? Own their own houses?
- Is family life important? Are seniors respected? Young children adored?
- What kind of recreation is popular? Sailing, swimming, theater, baseball?
- Do women work in offices, factories and the professions? Do they hold executive positions?
- What are the hours for doing business? Do people go home to eat lunch?
- How do business people greet one another?
- Do business people prize punctuality?
- Is someone's word his or her bond?
- Are business decisions made quickly?

When you have the answers to these and other questions you can better envision those with whom you interact. You'll accentuate similarities and probably feel more comfortable. You'll interpret business etiquette dictums appropriately. You won't, for example, feel slighted if your contact isn't punctual when you know his or her countrymen have a relaxed view regarding punctuality. Your personal comfort zone is important. When all is well, it will be easier for you to move ahead with confidence.

Casual Interest or Major Effort?

If you occasionally do business with people who are based in foreign countries, you'll probably enjoy reading the rest of this chapter to glean information and discover differences as well as similarities.

"For all knowledge and wonder (which is the seed of knowledge) is an impression of pleasure in itself."

Francis Bacon (*The Advancement of Learning*, 1605)

When you have a specific market in sight, you'll want to direct all your energies to mastery of that particular culture.

Some Sources of Information

Lesko's Info-Power II (Kensington, MD: Information USA, 1994) devotes twenty information-dense pages to the topic of "Selling Overseas: International Trade." You'll find a wealth of detailed information in this chapter. For example, it has a section titled "Cheap Office And Conference Space Overseas."

When business etiquette demands require that you and not your host arrange for a meeting room, catering services, and all the trimmings (e.g., mailings, translation services) it's helpful to know the American Embassy may be able to assist you. Lesko's directory helps you narrow your search by listing names, addresses, and telephone numbers of U.S. Department of Commerce Field Offices.

Here, too, is information about how to obtain "Foreign Country Background Notes" from the U.S. Government Printing Office in Washington [(202) 783-3238], for a small fee. These little publications offer information about a specific country's people, economy, history, and government. According to Lesko, you should also check with Public Affairs Bureau, U.S. Department of State for "Foreign Country Background Notes" at (202) 647-2518 to learn how to obtain these publications free of charge.

Department of State Background Notes are also available via the National Trade Data Bank (NTDB) a so-called Trade Information Library, which you may be able to access at your nearest Federal Depository Library. Call: (800) 872-8723 for further information. NTDB will generally be found in the government documents section of the library and a reference librarian should be able to assist you.

One "Culturgram" from Kennedy Center Publications, Brigham Young University in Provo, Utah [(800) 528-6279] is reproduced here with permission. Individual Culturgrams, which are four-page briefing papers, are available for countries from A to Z (i.e., Algeria to Zimbabwe). The publisher frequently updates material. Retail prices for individual Culturgrams are $3.00. Discounts apply for quantity purchases. The Center also publishes several "Infograms," which address intercultural topics.

CULTURGRAM™ '97

Japan

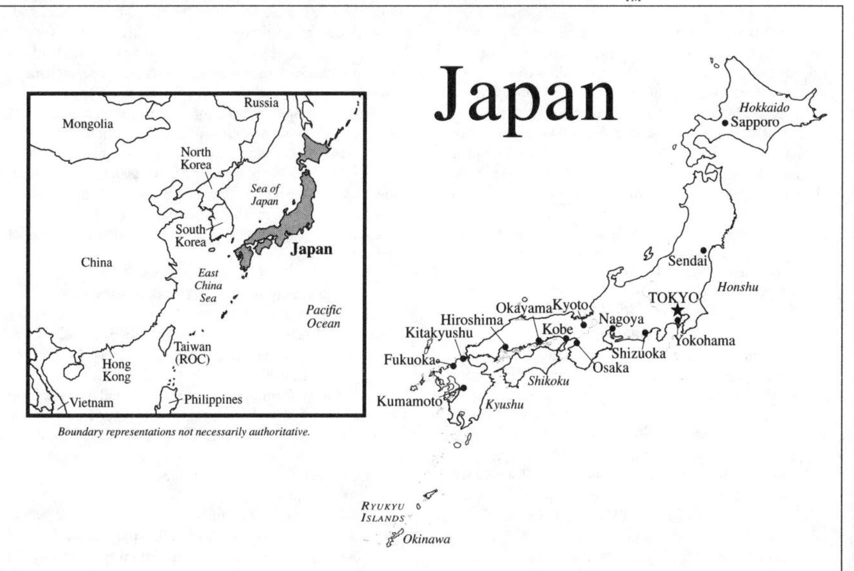

Boundary representations not necessarily authoritative.

BACKGROUND

Land and Climate

Japan consists of four main islands: Honshu, Hokkaido, Shikoku, and Kyushu. Covering 145,882 square miles (377,835 square kilometers), it is just smaller than Montana. Japan experiences all four seasons. On Hokkaido and in northern Honshu, winters can be bitterly cold. To the south, a more tropical climate prevails. Otherwise, the climate is temperate with warm, humid summers and mild winters. The western side of the islands is usually colder than the eastern side, which faces the Pacific Ocean. The islands are subject to typhoons in September. Japan also has many dormant and a few active volcanoes. Mild earthquakes are fairly common, and more destructive ones hit every few years. The January 1995 quake in and around Kobe killed more than five thousand people and was the worst of several quakes since a 1923 Tokyo quake that killed 140,000.

History

Japan is known historically as the "Land of the Rising Sun," as symbolized by its flag. Beginning more than two thousand years ago (with Emperor Jimmu in 600 B.C., according to legend), Japan has had a line of emperors that continues to the present. From the 12th century until the late 19th century, however, feudal lords or *Shoguns* held political control. These *Shoguns* expelled all foreigners in the 17th century on the suspicion they were spies for European armies. Not until 1853, when Matthew Perry (U.S. Navy) sailed into port, did the Japanese again have contact with the West. The *Shoguns* lost power in the 1860s and the emperor again took control. The current emperor, Akihito, took the throne in 1989. Akihito's father, Hirohito, was emperor from 1926 to 1989. Hirohito's reign was called *Showa*, which means "enlightened peace." The deceased Hirohito is now properly referred to as "Emperor Showa." Akihito's reign is called *Heisei*, meaning "achievement of universal peace."

Japan established itself as a regional power through military victories against China (1895) and Russia (1905). Involvement in World War I brought Japan enhanced global influence, and the Treaty of Versailles expanded its land holdings. The post-war years brought prosperity to the rapidly changing nation. It soon began to exercise considerable influence in Asia and subsequently invaded Manchuria and much of China. On 7 December 1941, Japan launched a successful air attack on U.S. naval forces at Pearl Harbor. Its military machine swiftly encircled most of Southeast Asia. But in 1943, the tide of the war turned against Japan. The United States dropped atomic bombs on Hiroshima and Nagasaki in the summer of 1945. Complete collapse of the empire and surrender ensued. A military occupation, chiefly by U.S. forces, lasted from 1945 to 1952. In 1947, Japan adopted a new constitution under American direction, renouncing war, granting basic human rights, and declaring

ASIA

Japan a democracy. The United States and Japan have since maintained close political and military ties despite periodic trade tensions.

Japan's post-war focus was on economic development and the country experienced rapid change and modernization. The Liberal Democratic Party (LDP) generally controlled politics after World War II, but scandals in the 1980s and early 1990s led to high-level resignations, splinter parties, and a weaker LDP. In 1993, it lost its majority and served as a coalition partner to the rival Socialist Party under Prime Minister Tomiichi Murayama. Newly appointed LDP leader Ryutaro Hashimoto restored his party to power when Murayama resigned in January 1996. As a coalition partner, the LDP did not have to stand for early elections in order for Hashimoto to become prime minister and govern until general elections scheduled for 1997.

THE PEOPLE

Population

Japan's population of 125.5 million is growing at 0.3 percent annually. Although Japan's population is half that of the United States, it resides on less than 5 percent of the total territory of the United States. Japan is therefore one of the most densely populated countries in the world. Nearly 80 percent of all people live in urban areas. About 45 percent are concentrated in three major metropolitan areas: Tokyo, Osaka, and Nagoya. Tokyo is the world's most populous city. Japan is 99 percent ethnic Japanese, with a small number of Koreans (about 680,000) and Chinese. Native Ainu live mostly on Hokkaido. All non-Japanese must register annually with the police and do not have full citizenship rights.

Japan's Human Development Index (0.937) ranks it third out of 173 countries. The ranking reflects a high level of economic and social organization, but it does not take into account Japan's high cost of living and the stress inherent in an emphasis on work, a lack of affordable housing, and inflexible social institutions. Adjusted for women, the index (0.896) ranks Japan eighth out of 130 nations. This rank accurately reflects Japanese women's inferior social status and limited access to resources that allow them to pursue personal goals as freely as men.

Language

Japanese is the official language. Although spoken Japanese is not closely related to spoken Chinese, the written language (kanji) is related to Chinese ideographs (characters), which were adopted in ancient times. The Japanese also use two phonetic alphabets (*hiragana* and *katakana*) simplified from these characters. A third phonetic alphabet (*romaji*) uses Roman letters. English is taught in all secondary schools and is often used in business. The Japanese also place great worth on nonverbal language or communication. For example, much can be said with a proper bow. In fact, one is often expected to sense another person's feelings on a subject without verbal communication. Some Westerners misinterpret this as a desire to be vague or incomplete. The Japanese may consider a person's inability to interpret feelings as insensitivity.

Religion

Traditionally, most Japanese practiced a combination of Buddhism and Shinto. Shinto has no recognized founder or central scripture but is based on ancient mythology. It stresses man's relationship to nature and its many gods. All Japanese emperors are considered literal descendants of the sun goddess, Amaterasu. Shinto was important historically in ordering Japanese social values, as illustrated by the Code of the Warrior (*Bushido*), which stressed honor, courage, politeness, and reserve.

Shinto principles of ancestor veneration, ritual purity, and a respect for nature's beauty are all obvious in Japanese culture. Many households observe some ceremonies of both Shinto and Buddhism, such as Shinto marriages and Buddhist funerals, and most have small shrines in their homes. For most, however, this is done more out of respect for social tradition than out of religious conviction. About 1 percent of the population is Christian.

General Attitudes

Japanese society is group oriented. Loyalty to the group (business, club, etc.) and to one's superiors is essential and takes precedence over personal feelings. In business, loyalty, devotion, and cooperation are valued over aggressiveness. Companies traditionally provide lifetime employment to the "salaryman" (full-time male professional), and the salaryman devotes long hours of work to the company. This tradition was undermined by the recession of the early 1990s but is still a pillar of society. Devotion to the group reaches all ages; even members of a youth baseball team will place the team's interests over their own.

Politeness is extremely important; a direct "no" is seldom given, but a phrase like "I will think about it" can mean "no." Also out of politeness, a "yes" may be given quickly, even though it only means the person is listening or understands the speaker's request. The Japanese feel a deep obligation to return favors and gifts. They honor age and tradition. Losing face or being shamed in public is very undesirable. *Gamam* (enduring patience) is a respected trait that carries one through personal hardship, but it has also been used to dismiss the need for social change.

Nevertheless, even as many traditions remain strong, Japan's rising generation is beginning to revise society's view of economic security, family relations, politics, and male and female roles.

Personal Appearance

Conformity, even in appearance, is a characteristic of the Japanese. The general rule is to act similar to, or in harmony with, the crowd. Businessmen wear suits and ties in public. Proper dress is necessary for certain occasions. Conformity takes on a different meaning for the youth, however. They will wear the latest fashions (U.S. American and European) and colors, as long as these fashions are popular. Traditional clothing, called a *kimono* or *wafuku*, is a long robe with long sleeves, wrapped with a special sash (*obi*). The designs in the fabric can be simple or elaborate. The *kimono* is worn for social events or special occasions.

CUSTOMS AND COURTESIES

Greetings

A bow is the traditional greeting between Japanese. Persons wishing to show respect or humility bow lower than the other person. The Japanese shake hands with Westerners.

While some appreciate it when Westerners bow, others do not, especially when the two people are not acquainted. Therefore, a handshake is most appropriate for foreign visitors. The Japanese are formal, and titles are important in introductions. A family name is used with the suffix *san*. A Mr. Ogushi in North America is called *Ogushi-san* in Japan. The use of first names is reserved for family and friends. Between business representatives, the exchange of business cards (offered and accepted with both hands) most often accompanies a greeting.

Greetings used depend on the relationship. A worker might greet a superior with *Ohayogozaimasu* (Good morning), but he or she would greet a customer with *Irasshaimase* (Welcome). When business representatives meet for the first time, they may use *Hajimemashite* (Nice to meet you). *Konnichiwa* (Hello) is a standard greeting. *Ohayoh* (an informal "Good morning"), *Yahhoh* (Hey!), or *Genki?* (How are you?) are common casual greetings among the youth.

Gestures

Yawning in public is impolite. A person should sit up straight with both feet on the floor. Legs may be crossed at the knee or ankles, but placing an ankle over a knee is improper. One beckons by waving all fingers with the palm down. It is polite to point with the entire hand. Shaking one hand from side to side with the palm forward means "no." A person refers to himself by pointing the index finger at his nose. Laughter does not necessarily signify joy or amusement; it can also be a sign of embarrassment. One covers one's mouth when using a toothpick. Chewing gum in public is considered impolite. Young girls often walk hand in hand.

Visiting

Visits usually are arranged in advance; spontaneous visits between neighbors are uncommon in urban areas. The Japanese remove shoes before stepping into a home. There is usually a small hallway (*genkan*) between the door and living area where one stands to remove the shoes and place them together pointing toward the outdoors—or in a closet or on a shelf in the *genkan*. People take off their coats before stepping into the *genkan*. Slippers are often worn inside but not in rooms with straw-mat floors (*tatami*). Japanese traditionally emphasize modesty and reserve. Guests usually are offered the most comfortable seat. When offered a meal, they often express slight hesitation before accepting it. Light refreshments are accepted graciously. The Japanese deny compliments out of modesty. Guests avoid excessive compliments on items in the home because they would embarrass the hosts.

Guests customarily take a gift (usually fruit or cakes) to their hosts. People give and accept gifts with both hands and a slight bow. Some, especially the elderly, may consider it impolite to open the gift right away. Gift giving is extremely important, especially in business, because a gift says a great deal about the giver's relationship to, and respect for, the recipient. Food and drink are the most common gifts, as gifts for the house would quickly clutter small homes. Gift giving reaches its peak at the end of each year, when giving the right-priced present (the price is more important than the item) to all the right people (family, friends, officials, and business contacts) sets the tone for the coming year.

Eating

Although many young people eat while walking in public, it is generally considered bad manners for adults to do so. Therefore, snack foods sold at street stands are eaten at the stand. In a traditional meal, the Japanese typically eat from their bowl while holding it at chest level instead of bending down to the table. People eat most meals with chopsticks (*hashi*), but they generally use Western utensils when eating Western food. U.S. American fast-food is popular among the youth. The main meal is eaten in the evening. Because many men work late hours, they may eat dinner in office-building restaurants or on the way home.

LIFESTYLE

Family

The family is the foundation of Japanese society and is bound together by a strong sense of reputation, obligation, and responsibility. A person's actions reflect on the family. Affection, time together, and spousal compatibility are less important than in other cultures. While the father is the head of the home, the mother is responsible for household affairs and raising children. Traditionally, it was considered improper for a woman to have a job, but many women now work outside the home. Divorce and single parenthood are rare compared to other nations, due mostly to economic pressures and negative stigmas associated with both. Families generally have fewer than three children. In cities, families live in high-rise apartments or small homes. Larger homes are found in less-crowded areas.

Dating and Marriage

Youth in Japan are much like youth in the United States. They begin dating at around age 15 and enjoy dancing, going to movies, shopping, or eating out. They like Western music and fashion trends. The average marriage age is 27 for men and 26 for women. Weddings can be elaborate and expensive. Marriage ceremonies usually take place in hotels. The couple may wear traditional *kimonos* for the ceremony, Western wedding outfits for photographs and socializing, and different clothing for an evening party. Wedding guests bring gifts, often cash, and leave with gifts from the couple.

Diet

The Japanese diet consists largely of rice, fresh vegetables, seafood, fruit, and small portions of meat. Rice and tea are part of almost every meal. Western-style food is increasingly popular, especially among the youth. Popular Japanese foods include *miso* (bean paste) soup, noodles (*raman*, *udon*, and *soba*), curried rice, *sashimi* (uncooked fish), tofu, and pork. Sushi is usually a combination of fish (cooked or raw) and rice, with vinegar. Sometimes a vegetable, such as cucumber, is added to the dish or used instead of fish; then the dish is called *norimaki*. Sushi is expensive and reserved for special occasions.

Recreation

Baseball, soccer, volleyball, tennis, skiing, and jogging are all popular in Japan. The Japanese also enjoy traditional sports such as sumo wrestling (a popular spectator sport), judo, *kendo* (fencing with bamboo poles), and karate. Baseball, brought to Japan in the 1870s by an American, is the national sport. It is highly competitive at all levels. The entire country follows the annual national high school championships. Golf, while expensive, is popular among men. For leisure, people enjoy television and movies or nature outings. Older adults favor puppet theater (*bunraku*) and highly stylized drama (*noh* and *kabuki*). The Japanese also attend music concerts and theater.

Holidays

At the New Year, Japanese take an extended holiday from the last day or two in December to about the third of January. Businesses and government offices close while people visit shrines and relatives. Other important holidays include Adults' Day (15 January), when those who will turn 20 during the year are honored as coming of age; National Foundation Day (11 February); Vernal Equinox (in March); *Midori No hi* (Greenery Day, 29 April), a day to celebrate nature's beauty; Constitution Day (3 May); Children's Day (5 May); Bon Festival (15 August), a time when people take vacation and return to their ancestral homes to welcome visiting ancestral spirits with bonfires; Respect for the Aged Day (15 September); Autumnal Equinox (in September); Sports Day (10 October); Culture Day (3 November); Labor Thanksgiving Day (23 November); and Emperor Akihito's Birthday (23 December).

Commerce

Businesses are typically open from 8:00 A.M. to 5:00 P.M. or 9:00 A.M. to 6:00 P.M. Small shops and large urban shopping areas may stay open much later and do not close for lunch. Business dealings are conducted formally. Time is often required for decisions and agreements. The Japanese may be more interested in the person or company they are dealing with than the actual details of the deal. Many Japanese work late into the evening; overtime is a common necessity.

SOCIETY

Government

Japan is a constitutional monarchy. The emperor is head of state but has no governing power. The prime minister is head of government. He and his cabinet form the executive branch. Legislative power is vested in the *Diet*, consisting of the 511-seat House of Representatives (lower house) and the 252-seat House of Councillors (upper house). Japan has 47 prefectures (provinces), each administered by an elected governor. The voting age is 20. In addition to the LDP, major parties include the Social Democratic Party of Japan, Democratic Socialist Party, and New Frontier Party.

Economy

Japan is one of the most productive industrialized nations in the world. Inflation and unemployment are less than 3 percent, and gross domestic product (GDP) growth is more than 2 percent. Real GDP per capita is $20,520. Because Japan has few natural resources, it depends on imported raw materials for industrial success. Also, because more than 60 percent of the land is mountainous, only about 13 percent is suitable for cultivation. Japan must import nearly half of its food supply, including grains other than rice. Major crops include rice, sugar, vegetables, tea, and various fruits. Japan is a leading producer of fish, accounting for 15 percent of the total world catch.

The economy is based on manufacturing. More than 95 percent of all exports are manufactured items, including automobiles, electronic equipment, televisions, and other items. Major industries include machinery, metals, engineering, electronics, textiles, and chemicals. The United States is Japan's biggest trading partner, but a trade imbalance and conflicts over market access are sources of friction between the two allies. Japan's *yen* (¥) is one of the world's strongest currencies.

Transportation and Communication

A highly developed, efficient mass-transit system of trains and buses is the principal mode of transportation in urban areas. "Bullet" trains (*Shinkansen*) provide rapid transportation between major cities. Subways are also available. Many people have private cars. Traffic is often heavy in Tokyo and other large cities. Japan has five international airports. Its communications system is highly modern and well developed. Newspapers and magazines are read by more than 65 million people.

Education

Japan has a high literacy rate (99 percent) and reading is popular. Education is generally free and compulsory from ages six to fifteen. Individuals must pay tuition for education thereafter. The curriculum stresses math and sciences. Students are in school Monday through Saturday, with one Saturday off a month. Many students attend private schools, provided they pass difficult entrance exams (even at the kindergarten level). Parents often enroll their children in *juku* (cram) schools to help them prepare for these tests. University entrance exams are rigorous, and competition among students is intense. Students study for years and cram for months to take them. Getting into the most prestigious schools is more important than one's ultimate performance. Graduation from the top universities usually guarantees students well-paying jobs. These universities are affiliated with specific high, middle, and elementary schools; hence, getting into the right elementary school can help guarantee one's future success.

Health

The Japanese enjoy one of the highest standards of health in the world. The infant mortality rate is only 4 per 1,000. Life expectancy is between 77 and 82 years. Companies are generally responsible for providing insurance benefits to employees, but the government also sponsors some social welfare programs. Medical facilities are very good. Pollution is a problem in Tokyo.

FOR THE TRAVELER

U.S. visitors need a valid passport but no visa for stays of fewer than 90 days. No immunizations are required. For detailed travel information, contact the Japan National Tourist Office, 1 Rockefeller Plaza, Suite 1250, New York, NY 10020; phone (212) 757–5640. You may also wish to contact the Embassy of Japan, 2520 Massachusetts Avenue NW, Washington, DC 20008.

Don't overlook information you may obtain by contacting a specific embassy. Ms. Marianne Stottrup Laursen, Commercial Attaché, Royal Danish Embassy, 3200 Whitehaven St., N.W., Washington, D.C. 20008-3683, [(202) 234-4300] can provide a comprehensive packet of information that includes, "Business Traveller's Guide '94, Copenhagen." As to matters of etiquette, the guide mentions that tipping is not customary in Denmark. Countless other useful bits of information are included. For example, the guide includes the observation that Copenhagen is an easy, comfortable city for a businesswoman. The guide comes complete with a map of the city.

Ask the embassy representative what kind of materials are available. At the Embassy of Japan, for example, a twenty-seven page booklet, "Negotiating with the Japanese—A Guide—1994" addresses questions of good manners and form as well as the topics pertaining to negotiation (e.g., the dangers of hidden agendas, taking a dispute to court). If you tell the embassy representative what you're looking for and why, you may discover a wealth of valuable information specific to your needs. (Japan Information And Culture Center, Embassy of Japan, Lafayette Centre, 1155 21st Street, N.W., Washington, D.C. 20036).

Trade & Culture, is a monthly magazine designed to "give executives ideas for practical use, by blending cultural insight into how-to articles." Call (800) 544-5684 for a sample copy or to arrange for a subscription.

Seminars that address the topic, "Globalization: Merging Strategy With Action," are available via Thunderbird, The American Graduate School of International Management, Glendale, Arizona, (602) 978-7925.

Who should attend? According to the school's literature most participants are management people with at least five years of experience and current job responsibilities that increasingly cross national borders.

One goal? "Increase you ability to manage cultural differences among and within your organization."

United Van Lines, Bette Malone Relocation Service, helps companies to assist employees who are relocating to other countries. Their cross-cultural training program is customized to needs of the relocating employee. A workbook and other materials are provided. The typical two-day seminar is divided into general information and country-specific information, including business and social etiquette. When time doesn't permit, a comprehensive written document can be prepared for employees moving to other cultures in lieu of conducting a cross-cultural training seminar. The American Culture Training program is available to foreign nationals moving to the United States.

Contact: United Van Lines, Inc., World Headquarters, One United Drive, Fenton, St. Louis, MO 63026 [(800) 325-3870] for further information, or contact the company that provides moving services for your company to learn whether a similar program is offered.

It's easy to see that once you begin to reach out for information it's not difficult to find. Be aware, however, that business etiquette information is often buried in the text of publications which attract your attention because "cross-cultural" or similar words are in their titles. Don't assume you'll find sufficient information to warrant making a purchase without first examining the publication or obtaining more details.

Nice Work If You Can Get It

Ms. Letitia Baldrige served as White House Chief of Staff for Jacqueline Kennedy, was social secretary to Ambassador David Bruce and special assistant to Ambassador Clare Boothe Luce. She has been called the "guru of social niceties" and "the doyenne of deportment."

Letitia Baldrige's Complete Guide to the New Manners for the '90s was re-released in November 1995. The following issues provide a sampling of material:

- What are the most supportive things you can say or do when you have a friend with AIDS?
- Is it appropriate to breast-feed in public?
- How should people introduce a partner of the same sex?

An earlier book, *Letitia Baldrige's New Complete Guide to Executive Manners*, was published in October 1993 and can be found at your library or neighborhood book store.

(If you haven't read the *Everyday Business Etiquette* Foreword, you may want to take a moment to do so. Ms. Baldrige graciously consented to write it for this author.)

Ms. Baldrige maintains a busy writing schedule but occasionally conducts etiquette seminars at the request of a company's executives. Call: (202) 328-1626 to discuss arrangements for a company seminar.

It's Not for Executives Only

A headline in *The Miami Herald*, dated Friday, October 7, 1994 reads: "Boomer generation that missed manners now sends its children to etiquette school."

The article discusses The Protocol School of Washington® located in the Washington, D.C. metropolitan area and Director, Ms. Dorothea Johnson, who operates the firm that provides private seminars and briefings on corporate etiquette, international etiquette, and cross-cultural awareness. Johnson instructs children and young adults as well as executives at Etiquette Camps conducted at a Palm Beach, Florida hotel each July.

A headline in *The Washington Post*, dated January 16, 1995 entitled "Getting It Right, The Latest Angle on Etiquette and Protocol," refers to Ms. Johnson and The Protocol School of Washington® as one resource for government officials, ambassadors, chief executive officers and celebrities who recognize they've got to "get it right" and need training and guidance in order to be successful.

Contact The Protocol School of Washington®, International Headquarters, 1401 Chain Bridge Road, Suite 202, McLean, Virginia 22101, (703) 821-5613 for information regarding services.

Speaking Out

Roger E. Axtell is a retired vice president, Worldwide Marketing, for the Parker Pen Company. He has spent thirty years living and traveling abroad. He's a popular after-dinner speaker on the subject of international business and behavior.

His books, published by John Wiley and Sons, include:

- *Do's and Taboos Around the World: A Guide to International Behavior, Third Edition*
- *Do's and Taboos of International Trade: A Small Business Primer*
- *Do's and Taboos of Hosting International Visitors*

Keep a Diary

> *"I never travel without my diary. One should always have something sensational to read in the train."*
>
> Oscar Wilde (*The Importance of Being Earnest, Act I*).

Since travel to conduct business with people in foreign countries invariably demands time spent en route, it makes good sense to keep a diary.

If you're as fine a recorder of events as Mr. Wilde's character, you may find it makes for sensational reading. At the least, it will serve to record your observations and provide you with a point of reference customized to your needs.

Devote a portion of the diary to times you entertain people who come from other countries to visit with you.

Here's how a diary delivers value:

- You can record someone's preferences (e.g., Christopher is a vegetarian), or dislikes (e.g., Georges is uncomfortable in places that feature loud music) and remember them next time you're together.
- If memory fails, your diary should reveal what gift you selected for the business person, his entourage, or children, so you can select a different gift the next time, or repeat a gift that made someone happy. The recipients aren't likely to forget and your efforts on their behalf aren't likely to go unappreciated.
- Create your own rating system for hotels, restaurants and other establishments you frequent. Use it as a guide when you plan your next trip. Record the names of a concierge, translator, or others who provided excellent service. You make a person feel appreciated when you address him or her by name upon your return. Moreover, you may want to engage some service provider again and it's easier to do when you have all necessary information.
- When you peruse your notes and comments, you may notice a recurring theme you didn't notice earlier or make another useful discovery. This often happens to reporters who tape an interview and replay the interview soon afterward. By listening to the information twice, some new insight often becomes apparent. Your diary will make it possible for you to experience a replay and perhaps expand your knowledge base. If, for example, an unobtrusive member of the other group's negotiating team attended every meeting, it could be the individual is more powerful than you've been led to understand. You may decide to favor this individual with more eye contact, conversation, invitations, or gifts. He or she may be the person you need to impress in order to achieve your business goals.

LEARNING FROM TIDBITS AND TEASES

The following information is thought to be accurate. This author has not yet had the privilege of conducting business in all of the following countries and accordingly can't vouch for the precision of the information regarding customs and practices.

May this admission serve to remind you that you must accept information as only being "probable" when it comes to determining how best to conduct business with people in or from other countries and cultures. Within each country there will be variations on a theme since people are not all alike. Generalizations are reasonable starting points but it's prudent to tread lightly until you can light the path with your very own lamp!

How enlightened are you? Your responses to the following tidbits and teases should provide clues:

(1) In **Jordan,** business meetings get underway

a. Immediately.

b. Once dark-roasted sugary Bedouin coffee has been served and consumed.

c. Only at the office, never at someone's home.

Good to know: Jordanian business travelers might engage lodgings for a week while their U.S. counterparts engage lodgings for two days in order to accomplish the same goals. What does this suggest? Jordanians and people from other Arab countries don't get down to business immediately! They're known for providing lavish hospitality to all, including newcomers, and therefore none of the above choices are appropriate.

(2) How do you attain "inner circle" status in **Japan?**

a. In order to be accepted as one who is inside *(uchi)* as opposed to outside (*soto*), a person must be powerful.

b. You're born into it.

c. It takes a long time to build good relationships and be accepted into the *uchi* circle.

Good to know: The answer is c. Japanese business people tend to favor insiders and many foreign business people imagine they'll never climb out of the *soto* circle simply because they're not Japanese. A mastery of business etiquette advances your position but the process is slow. This reality is not unique to Japan, though, as you may have experienced it in your own dealings in the United States.

(3) Should you pack formal attire when you travel to **Australia** to conduct business?

a. Pack according to the dictates of the business agenda but leave pretentious behavior at home. Australians are frank and direct.

b. Clothing is not as important as your punctuality.

c. If you blunder, your Australian business associates are likely to make light of it since they have a good sense of humor.

Good to know: The answer is all of the above. Australians prize punctuality and if you commit some social gaffes (i.e., dress inappropriately), they're likely to tease you since they're warm and friendly people. They know a lot about the United States and you'll score points when you demonstrate you know a good deal about them and their country.

(4) In **Mozambique,** when you meet a business contact you should:

a. Announce your first name and take a bow.

b. Show your interest in regional disputes.

c. Never talk about culture.

Good to know: The answer is none of the above. People rarely use first names, refrain from discussing regional disputes or politics with business contacts, and enjoy talking about history and culture.

(5) If a **Russian** business associate kisses your cheek, you know you have offended him.

a. Wrong. Bear hugs and kissing a person's cheeks are common displays of affection between friends.

b. True. Since most Russians don't speak English, this gesture is meant to send you a message you shouldn't ignore.

c. You're a candidate for a kiss on the cheek when you bring a gift of music albums or books.

Good to know: The answer is both a and c. By the way, many Russians speak some English.

(6) If a **Norwegian** business contact refers to you by your first name, it's because:

a. He or she probably knows a great deal about your customs.

b. Your Norwegian business contact has difficulty pronouncing your last name.

c. Norwegians tend to be more casual than people from the United States.

Good to know: The answer is a. Norwegians typically use last names only and hesitate to use first names. This contact is working to make you feel comfortable! On the whole, Norwegians are far less casual than their counterparts in the United States.

(7) Your **Belgian** business contact will snap his fingers when:

a. He's concentrating on what you say.

b. You arrive late.

c. Someone opens a door without knocking.

Good to know: The answer is c. Finger-snapping during the course of conversation is considered a rude gesture and your contact isn't likely to be rude. Don't arrive late because punctuality is appreciated. Privacy is valued, too, which accounts for the finger-snapping.

(8) When you're invited to dinner by a business contact in **Hong Kong:**

a. He'll lose face if you refuse, so suggest an alternate date or time if you're unable to accept the initial invitation.

b. Your Chinese host is trying to be pleasant but doesn't expect you to accept the invitation.

c. Don't expect him to talk about business.

Good to know: The answer is a. Business deals are often made at the dinner table.

(9) **New Zealand** business people don't like to discuss who has which business rank (i.e., top management, middle management). As a result:

a. It's difficult to know who can make final decisions.

b. Include all your primary contacts when you extend a dinner invitation since that's the customary time to discuss business.

c. Take note of who presents you with a gift at your first meeting. That person probably has the most power.

Good to know: The answer is a. New Zealand business people are reluctant to discuss who has power when they're in a group setting. If you must ask about rank, do so privately. Business is discussed at lunch, not dinner, and gifts are not exchanged the first time people meet.

(10) If you're invited to a **Chinese** banquet:

a. Don't expect rice to be served.

b. The host will expect to be praised but will apologize for not doing more.

c. No one notices whether or not you eat the food.

Good to know: The answer is b. A Chinese banquet isn't the same as an ordinary meal and rice isn't a featured food. It may be served at the end of the banquet and if you eat a large serving of rice you'll make it appear the host didn't provide sufficient meats, and so on. Be generous with your praise for the food. It's considered the polite thing to do.

(11) When doing business in **South Korea** men should:

a. Wear dark suits

b. Remove shoes at the door when entering any building

c. Skip the tie

Good to know: The answer is a. A dark suit, white shirt, and tie is appropriate dress for a businessman. A businesswoman is advised to dress conservatively, too, and refrain from wearing tight skirts since people often sit on the floor in restaurants and in their homes. Plan to remove your shoes before entering a temple or someone's house.

(12) **Japanese** business people hand out business cards:

a. Rarely

b. All the time

c. And expect you to offer one in return

Good to know: The answer is b and c. Business cards are popular when the potential for conducting business is promising and the flip side of a card is often printed in another language (hopefully English). It's rude to take a card and not give one in return. When you present your business card, make sure your name is right side up and accessible to the recipient for perusal.

(13) **Swiss** business people value courtesy and

a. they believe it's courteous to conduct business within their own provinces or canons.

b. they won't accept a drink without offering a toast.

c. they'll discuss any subject you care to discuss.

Good to know: The answer is none of the above. It's a trilingual (Swiss/German, Italian, French) nation where English is widely spoken and business people can function everywhere. Since courtesy is highly prized, c is especially inaccurate. Swiss business people arrive on time to keep appointments and expect others to be punctual, too. They're proud of their independence and high standard of living and too courteous to approve of displays of wealth.

(14) Business offices in **Italy** are open until 8:00 P.M.,

a. And business is conducted six days a week.

b. But many legal holidays are observed when entire cities close shop.

c. Yet business people won't agree to meet you to conduct business unless you've been introduced at an earlier date.

Good to know: The answer is a and b. Most firms close for vacation during the month of August and close for numerous holidays. Many firms offer three-hour lunch periods but companies conduct business on Saturdays and maintain early evening hours during the week. Italian business people are reluctant to deal with people they've never met and prefer a third party introduction.

(15) When in **Hong Kong,** don't forget the importance of:

a. Bowing when you greet someone.

b. Shaking hands only when you know a person well.

c. Shaking hands both when greeting and when saying goodbye.

Good to know: The answer is c. People in Hong Kong are reserved and consider it polite to shake hands both when greeting colleagues or taking leave.

(16) When you dine at a restaurant with a citizen of **Iceland,** you'll notice that when it comes to tipping:

a. Tips are small.

b. A 20 percent gratuity is automatically added to the cost of the meal.

c. No tip is ever left.

Good to know: The answer is c. Keep your money in your wallet since tipping in Iceland is not considered to be polite!

(17) **Australian** business people are very friendly but don't be late for an appointment since they find such behavior unpardonable.

a. Punctuality is prized.

b. Don't expect your Australian associate to "read" the clock the same way you do. Fifteen minutes more or less is still considered "on time."

c. The friendly, relaxed manner of the Australians can be disarming but good manners are highly valued.

Good to know: Blot out statement b. Focus on statement a. Who can argue with statement c? No one.

(18) When you're in **Puerto Rico,**

a. Gift giving is customary and the recipient is expected to politely decline the gift before finally accepting it.

b. Gift giving is of no particular importance but if you receive a gift take care to open it immediately.

c. Never go to a business meeting without bringing a gift along.

Good to know: The answer is b. Gift giving is common but the practice is not cast in stone. Do open a gift without delay and do say thank you. Say it in Spanish, and you're likely to delight your associate even though he or she speaks English well.

(19) When dining in **Mexico,**

a. Don't put your elbows on the table or stretch while seated at the dining table, either.

b. Mind all your table manners since business people in Mexico equate good manners with gentility and gentility is admired.

c. Don't make the mistake of thinking that exceedingly warm weather in Mexico excuses a man from wearing his jacket and tie when he dines. It doesn't!

Good to know: The answer is all of the above.

(20) Throughout the **United States,** a smile is customary when people greet one another. What else is true of greetings?

a. In some localities, normal eye contact is considered too intense and people look away to show respect.

b. Think twice about giving expensive gifts when you meet someone, since tax laws put a burden on your recipient when gifts received exceed $25.

c. When you offer your business card to someone, don't consider it a sign of displeasure if he or she doesn't offer you one in return.

Good to know: The answer is all of the above. Alone, these facts are of small value but along with other information, they give a person's confidence level a boost when he or she must conduct business with people in the United States. This last exercise is presented to remind you that a little know-how is welcome, but a heaping portion of know-how propels you up the ladder of success.

Happy climbing!

Index